Steck-Vaughn

Passwords
to English Grammar

An ESL Program for Spanish Speakers

Book
2

Betty Clare Moffatt

Consultants

Alice Contreras

Gabriel Cortina

Auturo McDonald

**Steck-Vaughn
Company**

A Subsidiary of National Education Corporation

TABLE OF CONTENTS

SECTION I
Classroom Verbs

1. The Past Tense

Here is an English verb conjugated in the past tense. This tense in English usually corresponds to the *pretérito* in Spanish.

I learned
you learned
he, she, it learned
we learned
you learned
they learned

To form the past tense of *to learn*, we add *ed* to the basic verb form (the infinitive without the *to*). Notice that in English we need to learn only one form for the past tense. In Spanish we have to learn several forms.

Study the sentences below. Repeat the sentences with your teacher.

I **learned** the new words.
You **learned** the English sentences.
He **learned** the words yesterday.
She **learned** the verbs quickly.
(It) The dog **learned** to obey.
We **learned** English last year.
They **learned** a new skill.

EXERCISE 1

Fill in each blank with the correct form of *to learn* in the past tense.

1. I _____ to speak English.

2. You _____ many new words.

3. Carlos _____ new expressions.

4. The teacher _____ Spanish in Mexico.

SECCIÓN I
Verbos de la Clase

1. El Pretérito

Aquí está un verbo en inglés conjugado en el tiempo pasado. Este tiempo en inglés usualmente corresponde al pretérito en español.

aprendí
aprendiste
aprendió
aprendimos
aprendisteis
aprendieron

Para formar el pretérito de *to learn*, se añade *ed* a la forma básica del verbo (el infinitivo sin el *to*). Note que en inglés, necesitamos aprender solamente una forma para el pretérito. En español tenemos que aprender varias formas.

Estudie las oraciones de abajo. Repita las oraciones con su maestra o maestro.

EJERCICIO 1

Llene cada espacio con la forma correcta de *to learn* en el pretérito.

5. We _____ the past tense in English.

6. They _____ about credit.

EXERCISE 2

Change the following sentences from the present to the past tense.

EJERCICIO 2

Cambie las siguientes oraciones del presente al pretérito.

1. We learn mathematics in school.

---

2. She learns how to operate the machine.

---

3. I learn how to measure correctly.

---

4. They learn how to fill out the application forms.

---

5. We learn how to speak English.

---

6. I learn how to use those tools.

---

7. Diana learns very quickly.

---

8. Alberto and Mike learn how to swim.

---

9. I learn bookkeeping.

---

10. We learn how to shop wisely.

---

11. You learn faster than the others.

---

2. Subject Pronouns

I (first person singular)
you (second person singular)

he (third person singular)
she (third person singular
it (third person singular)
we (first person plural)

you (second person plural)

they (third person plural)

USAGE

In English we use a subject pronoun or a noun with the verb to make a sentence. Notice the differences in the English and Spanish pronouns above.

In English we use the word *you* to indicate *tú, Ud., Uds., vosotros,* or *vosotras*.

The word *it* is used in English to indicate a thing or an animal—not a person.

EXAMPLE (EJEMPLO):
The parrot learned Spanish.
It learned Spanish.

They is the plural of *it. They* is used to indicate more than one object, animal, or person.

EXAMPLES (EJEMPLOS):
The dogs learned new tricks.
They learned new tricks.

The students learned English.
They learned English.

Go back to Lesson 1 and study the conjugation of *to learn* and the subject pronouns.

2. Los Pronombres Sujetos

yo (primera persona singular)
tú (segunda persona singular)
usted (Ud.) (tercera persona singular)
él (tercera persona singular)
ella (tercera persona singular)
— (no hay forma en español)
nosotros, (primera persona
nosotras plural)
vosotros, (segunda persona
vosotras plural)
ustedes (tercera persona plural)
(Uds.)
ellos, ellas (tercera persona plural)

USO

En inglés se usa un pronombre sujeto o un nombre con el verbo para formar una oración. Fíjese en las diferencias entre los pronombres ingleses y españoles de arriba.

En inglés se usa la palabra *you* para indicar *tú, Ud., Uds., vosotros,* o *vosotras.*

La palabra *it* se usa en inglés para indicar una cosa o un animal—nunca una persona.

They es el plural de *it. They* se usa para indicar más de una cosa, un animal, o una persona.

Regrese a Lección 1 y estudie la conjugación de *to learn* y los pronombres sujetos.

Notice that you normally have to use a subject pronoun or a noun with the verb to make a sentence in English. In Spanish this is not necessary.

Fíjese que normalmente se tiene que usar un pronombre sujeto o un nombre con el verbo para hacer una oración en inglés. En español esto no es necesario.

SENTENCES

Here are some sentences using the subject pronouns and *to learn* in the past tense. Repeat the sentences with your teacher. Note especially the subject pronouns.

ORACIONES

Aquí están algunas oraciones usando los pronombres sujetos y *to learn* en el pretérito. Repita las oraciones con su maestra o maestro. Note especialmente los pronombres sujetos.

> She **learned** English.
> They **learned** the lesson.
> We **learned** mathematics.
> You **learned** very little.
> He **learned** Spanish.

EXERCISE

Rewrite the following sentences by using a subject pronoun instead of the italicized noun or nouns.

EJERCICIO

Escriba de nuevo las siguientes oraciones usando un pronombre sujeto en lugar del nombre o nombres en letra itálica.

1. *Lupe* learned how to dance.

   ----

2. *Robert and Chris* learned Spanish.

   ----

3. *The parrot* learned how to whistle.

   ----

4. *Ruby* learned how to fix her car.

   ----

5. *Raul* learned the song.

   ----

6. *Nancy and Gilbert* learned French.

   ----

3. Regular Verbs

3. Verbos Regulares

INFINITIVES AND PAST FORMS

INFINITIVOS

to listen	listened
to repeat	repeated
to talk	talked
to translate	translated

escuchar
repetir
hablar
traducir

These are the infinitives and past forms of regular verbs. Verbs are called regular when the past tense is formed by adding an *ed* or *d* to the basic verb form.

Estos son los infinitivos y pretéritos de verbos regulares. Verbos se llaman regulares cuando el pretérito se forma con añadir *ed* o *d* a la forma básica del verbo.

EXAMPLES (EJEMPLOS):
learn   learned
move   moved

SENTENCES

ORACIONES

Repeat these sentences with your teacher.

Repita estas oraciones con su maestra o maestro.

I **talked** to the teacher.
We **repeated** the sentences.
She **talked** about her new car.
They **repeated** the words.
He **translated** the English words perfectly
We **listened** to the concert.
Javier **translated** the story into Spanish.
Judy and Larry **listened** to the news.

EXERCISE

EJERCICIO

Fill in each blank with the correct form of the verb.

Llene cada espacio con la forma correcta del verbo.

1. The teacher _____ to the students.
   hablό

2. Armando _____ the lesson.
   repitió

3. The dog _____ for a noise.
   escuchό

4. You _____ too much in class.
   hablό

5. She _____ the poem into French.
   tradujo

4. More Regular Verbs

4. Más Verbos Regulares

INFINITIVES AND PAST FORMS

INFINITIVOS

to correct	corrected
to test	tested
to remember	remembered
to study	studied

corregir
probar
acordarse, recordar
estudiar

Notice that the *y* in *study* is dropped and *ied* is added in forming the past tense. Many regular verbs ending in *y* form the past tense this way, but there are exceptions (see Lesson 22).

Note que la *y* en *study* se elimina y se añade *ied* para formar el pretérito. Muchos verbos regulares que terminan en *y* forman el pretérito en esta manera, pero hay excepciones (fíjese en Lección 22).

SENTENCES

ORACIONES

Repeat with your teacher.

Repita con su maestro o maestra.

They **tested** each other with the new words.
He **studied** all night.
We **remembered** the numbers.
I **studied** mathematics.
Hilda **remembered** the words to the song.
The teacher **corrected** my pronunciation.
You **tested** the water.
I **corrected** the spelling errors.
They **remembered** to bring their pencils.
We **studied** very little.

EXERCISE 1

EJERCICIO 1

Change the following sentences from the present to the past tense.

Cambie las siguientes oraciones del presente al pretérito.

1. Mario corrects his mistakes.

----

2. I study French.

----

3. Elaine remembers his name.

----

4. He tests the new car.

----

5. You study history.

---

6. We remember to sign our names.

---

7. The teacher tests the students.

---

8. They study at the library.

---

9. I remember the answer.

---

10. We correct our own mistakes.

EXERCISE 2

Write sentences using the past tense of each of the following verbs at least once: *to correct, to test, to remember, and to study.*

EJERCICIO 2

Escriba oraciones usando el pretérito de cada uno de los siguientes verbos a lo menos una vez: *to correct, to test, to remember,* y *to study.*

1. _____

2. _____

3. _____

4. _____

5. _____

6. _____

7. _____

8. _____

5. Irregular Verbs

5. Verbos Irregulares

INFINITIVES AND PAST FORMS

INFINITIVOS

to know	knew	saber	
to speak	spoke	hablar	
to read	read	leer	
to say	said	decir	
to tell	told	decir	

These are irregular verbs. Certain verbs are called irregular because we do not add *ed* or *d* to form the past tense. Instead the verb changes its form or sometimes does not change at all.

Estos son verbos irregulares. Ciertos verbos se llaman irregulares porque no añadimos *ed* o *d* para formar el pretérito. En lugar de esto, el verbo cambia su forma o a veces no se cambia en ningún modo.

Here is an irregular verb conjugated in the past tense.

Aquí está un verbo irregular conjugado en el pretérito.

I knew
you knew
he, she, it knew
we knew
you knew
they knew

Notice that irregular verbs, like regular verbs, have only one form in the past tense. This form must be memorized for each irregular verb.

Note que verbos irregulares, como verbos regulares, tienen no más una forma en el pretérito. Esta forma se tiene que aprender de memoria por cada verbo irregular.

SENTENCES

ORACIONES

Repeat these sentences with your teacher.

Repita estas oraciones con su maestro o maestra.

You **read** the lesson very well.
She **read** her book.
Richard **spoke** slowly.
Elena **said** all the words correctly.
They **spoke** with their teacher.
I **knew** the song.
He **knew** about the accident.
We **said** our prayers.
He **told** us about his trip.
Frank **told** the children a story.

EXERCISE 1

Fill in each blank with the correct form of the verb.

EJERCICIO 1

Llene cada espacio con la forma correcta del verbo.

1. She _____ the newspaper.
   leyó

2. He _____ us to go home.
   dijo

3. Eduardo and Luisa _____ with the owner of
   hablaron
   the house.

4. She _____ the answer.
   dijo

5. I _____ where to go.
   supe

6. They _____ him to leave.
   dijeron

EXERCISE 2

Change the following sentences from the present to the past.

EJERCICIO 2

Cambie las siguientes oraciones del presente al pretérito.

1. I speak with my doctor.

   ----

2. She knows the time.

   ----

3. We say the vocabulary words.

   ----

4. David reads the sign by the window.

   ----

5. I tell him how to write it.

   ----

6. She reads very quickly.

   ----

6. More Irregular Verbs

6. Más Verbos Irregulares

INFINITIVES AND PAST FORMS

INFINITIVOS

to write	wrote
to teach	taught
to understand	understood
to forget	forgot

escribir
enseñar
entender
olvidarse

These are irregular verbs. Study their past tenses.

Estos son verbos irregulares. Estudie los pretéritos.

SENTENCES

ORACIONES

Repeat these sentences with your teacher.

Repita estas oraciones con su maestra o maestro.

Henry **forgot** the words.
You **taught** me how to dance.
Linda **wrote** a message to her friends.
I **understood** the story.
(It) The dog **understood** its owner.
They **wrote** letters from Mexico.
The teacher **taught** the English verbs to the class.
I **forgot** my notebook.

EXERCISE 1

EJERCICIO 1

Write sentences using the past tense of each of the following verbs at least once: *to write, to teach, to understand,* and *to forget.*

Escriba oraciones usando el pretérito de cada uno de los siguientes verbos a lo menos una vez: *to write, to teach, to understand,* y *to forget.*

1. _____

2. _____

3. _____

4. _____

5. _____

6. _____

7. _____

8. _____

EXERCISE 2

Change the following sentences to the past tense.

EJERCICIO 2

Cambie las siguientes oraciones al pretérito.

1. She writes a very good story.

   ----

2. He teaches Spanish in high school.

   ----

3. We forget to bring our umbrellas.

   ----

4. Lucy understands everything.

   ----

5. I teach them how to swim.

   ----

6. They write in their workbooks.

   ----

7. Lupe understands the instructions.

   ----

8. I forget his name.

   ----

9. He writes a letter to his family.

   ----

10. You forget the answer.

    ----

7. To Be

7. Estar y Ser

CONJUGATION

I was
you were
he, she, it was
we were
you were
they were

CONJUGACIONES

estuve   fui
estuviste   fuiste
estuvo   fue
estuvimos   fuimos
estuvisteis   fuisteis
estuvieron   fueron

SENTENCES

To be is irregular in the past tense in English. There are two forms to learn, *was* and *were*. Study the conjugations carefully and then repeat the sentences below with your teacher.

I **was** a carpenter in Mexico.
You **were** my friend.
He **was** a good man.
It **was** a nice day yesterday.
We **were** students last year.
They **were** right.

Was and *were* are sometimes used in questions.

EXAMPLES (EJEMPLOS):
Was it very dark out there?
Were you at the meeting this morning?

ORACIONES

To be es irregular en el pretérito en inglés. Hay dos formas para aprender, *was* y *were*. Estudie las conjugaciones cuidadosamente y luego repita las oraciones de abajo con su maestra o maestro.

Was y *were* se usan a veces en preguntas.

EXERCISE 1

Fill in the blanks with *was* or *were*.

EJERCICIO 1

Llene los espacios con *was* o *were*.

1. She _____ at home.

2. We _____ very cold.

3. The teacher _____ at a meeting.

4. The room _____ very clean.

5. They _____ at the office.

6. The books _____ on top of the desk.

7. He _____ a good actor.

EXERCISE 2

Write sentences using the word *was*.

EJERCICIO 2

Escriba oraciones usando la palabra *was*.

1. _____
2. _____
3. _____
4. _____
5. _____
6. _____
7. _____
8. _____
9. _____
10. _____
11. _____

EXERCISE 3

Write sentences using the word *were*.

EJERCICIO 3

Escriba oraciones usando la palabra *were*.

1. _____
2. _____
3. _____
4. _____
5. _____
6. _____
7. _____
8. _____
9. _____
10. _____
11. _____

8. Negative Sentences with To Be

8. Oraciones Negativas con Estar y Ser

NEGATIVES

Here are some negative sentences with *was* and *were*. Repeat with your teacher.

> She **was** not hungry.
> The answers **were** not correct.
> It **was** not cold outside.
> We **were** not home.
> He **was** not inside the house.

NEGATIVOS

Aquí están unas oraciones negativas con *was* y *were*. Repita con su maestro o maestra.

CONTRACTIONS

Wasn't is the contraction of *was* and *not*, and *weren't* is the contraction of *were* and *not*. Repeat with your teacher.

> They **were**n't at the dance.
> It **was**n't very smooth.
> I **was**n't angry.
> We **were**n't tired yet.
> You **were**n't very friendly.

Wasn't and *weren't* can also be used for negative questions.

> EXAMPLES (EJEMPLOS):
> Weren't you at the fiesta last night?
> Wasn't the book over there yesterday?

CONTRACCIONES

Wasn't es la contracción de *was* y *not*, y *weren't* es la contracción de *were* y *not*. Repita con su maestra o maestro.

Wasn't y *weren't* también se pueden usar para preguntas negativas.

EXERCISE 1

Change the following sentences to the negative. Use the word *not*.

1. She was happy.

----

2. Pablo and Julia were at the dance last night.

EJERCICIO 1

Cambie las siguientes oraciones al negativo. Use la palabra *not*.

3. I was very ill.

----

4. We were at the office yesterday morning.

EXERCISE 2

Change the following sentences and questions to the negative. Use the contraction *wasn't* or *weren't*.

EJERCICIO 2

Cambie las siguientes oraciones y preguntas al negativo. Use la contracción *wasn't* o *weren't*.

1. Was it on the floor?

----

2. It was very dark outside.

----

3. Were you home yesterday afternoon?

----

4. You were very cheerful.

EXERCISE 3

Cross out the incorrect word.

EJERCICIO 3

Tache la palabra incorrecta.

1. We (were, was) not at the meeting.
2. She (wasn't, weren't) very ill.
3. I (was, were) not thirsty.
4. They (weren't, wasn't) very expensive.
5. You (were, was) not at your office.

INFINITIVE CROSSWORD PUZZLE

Fill in the blanks with the verbs in English.

CRUCIGRAMA DE INFINITIVOS

Llene los espacios con los verbos en inglés.

HORIZONTAL

1. repetir
4. aprender
5. estar
6. probar
7. leer
10. estudiar
11. olvidarse

VERTICAL

1. recordar
2. hablar
3. corregir
8. entender
9. decir

Review of Section I

Repaso de Sección I

EXERCISE 1

Here is a list of the verbs in Section One. Next to each verb, write the past tense form of the verb. Then write **R** if the verb is regular or **I** if it is irregular.

EJERCICIO 1

Aquí está una lista de los verbos de Sección Una. Escriba el pretérito al lado de cada verbo. Luego escriba una **R** si el verbo es regular o una **I** si es irregular.

1. to learn
2. to know
3. to speak
4. to talk
5. to say
6. to tell
7. to read
8. to write
9. to listen
10. to repeat
11. to study
12. to teach
13. to translate
14. to correct
15. to test
16. to understand
17. to forget
18. to remember

EXERCISE 2

Fill in each blank with the correct form of the verb.

EJERCICIO 2

Llene cada espacio con la forma correcta del verbo.

1. He _____ a letter to his parents.
   escribió

2. She _____ to bring my pencil.
   <u>se le olvidó</u>

3. Murray and Lucy _____ their words.
   <u>estudiaron</u>

4. She _____ the note into Spanish.
   <u>tradujo</u>

5. They _____ the story together.
   <u>leyeron</u>

6. Edward _____ president of the club last year.
   <u>fue</u>

7. We _____ to the music.
   <u>escuchamos</u>

8. He _____ me the answer.
   <u>dijo</u>

9. Elsa _____ to bring her umbrella.
   <u>se acordó</u>

10. It _____ very cold outside.
   <u>estuvo</u>

EXERCISE 3

Change the following sentences to the past tense.

EJERCICIO 3

Cambie las siguientes oraciones al pretérito.

1. She understands the instructions.

   ----

2. We study for the test.

   ----

3. She teaches mathematics.

   ----

4. Raul and Marta talk over the phone.

   ----

5. I know the answer.

   ----

6. You speak very softly.

   ----

7. The sign says, "No Smoking."

SECTION II
Verbs of Daily Activities

9. Regular Verbs

INFINITIVES AND PAST FORMS

to wash	washed
to bathe	bathed
to dry	dried
to clean	cleaned

SENTENCES

Repeat these sentences with your teacher.

Gloria and I **washed** all the windows.
They **cleaned** their room.
She **bathed** the baby carefully.
You **dried** the dishes.
He **bathed** his dog.
Carlos **cleaned** the yard.
Larry **washed** his clothes.
The lemons **dried** up.
We **washed** our car.

You can use *washed* to describe the act of washing people, animals or things. You can use *bathed* to describe the act of washing people or animals only—not things.

EXERCISE 1

Change these sentences to the past tense.

1. We wash our hands.

----

2. Silvia bathes her feet in hot water.

SECCIÓN II
Verbos de Actividades Diarias

9. Verbos Regulares

INFINITIVOS

lavar, lavarse
bañarse
secar
limpiar

ORACIONES

Repita estas oraciones con su maestro o maestra.

Puede usar *washed* para describir el acto de lavar gente, animales, o cosas. Puede usar *bathed* para describir el acto de lavar gente o animales no más—no cosas.

EJERCICIO 1

Cambie estas oraciones al pretérito.

3. Manuel dries the corn shucks in the sun.

----

4. I clean my desk.

----

5. They dry their hands with the paper towels.

----

6. Mike cleans his glasses.

----

7. They dry their clothes in the dryer.

----

8. You clean this very well.

EXERCISE 2

Write sentences using the past tense of each of the following verbs at least once: *to wash, to bathe, to dry*, and *to clean*.

EJERCICIO 2

Escriba oraciones usando el pretérito de cada uno de los siguientes verbos a lo menos una vez: *to wash, to bathe, to dry*, y *to clean*.

1. --

2. --

3. --

4. --

5. --

6. --

10. More Regular Verbs

10. Más Verbos Regulares

INFINITIVES AND PAST FORMS

INFINITIVOS

to cook	cooked
to rest	rested
to help	helped

cocinar
descansar
ayudar

SENTENCES

ORACIONES

Repeat with your teacher.

Repita con su maestra o maestro.

We **cooked** dinner.
The cat **rested** in the shade.
We **rested** for a while.
He **helped** me with my homework.
Sara **cooked** the rice.
They **helped** us move the table.

EXERCISE

EJERCICIO

Fill in each blank with the correct form of *to cook*, *to rest*, or *to help* in the past tense.

Llene cada espacio con la forma correcta de *to cook*, *to rest*, o *to help* en el pretérito.

1. Juan _____ us open the windows.

2. We _____ after all that work.

3. She _____ me find the word in the dictionary.

4. He _____ breakfast this morning.

5. I _____ on the sofa.

6. Mike and I _____ the corn.

7. We _____ the chicken in the oven.

8. They _____ after crossing the river.

9. The glasses _____ him to read better.

10. Pablo _____ me lift it.

11. Celia _____ for an hour in her room.

12. You _____ it too long.

11. Irregular Verbs

11. Verbos Irregulares

INFINITIVES AND PAST FORMS

to make   made
to eat   ate
to drink   drank

INFINITIVOS

hacer
comer
beber

SENTENCES

Study the verb forms above. Repeat these sentences with your teacher.

ORACIONES

Estudie las formas de los verbos de arriba. Repita estas oraciones con su maestra o maestro.

> I **made** a chair in my workshop.
> Jerry **drank** all the lemonade.
> I **made** a kite with the paper.
> He **drank** it very quickly.
> She **ate** half of the apple.
> You **ate** too much at the party.

IDIOMS

Made is often used in idioms. An idiom is a group of words that has a special meaning. It is very difficult or sometimes impossible to understand this meaning by studying the words separately. You have to memorize the meaning of each idiom as a whole.

EXAMPLES (EJEMPLOS):
She made the bus just in time.
The story made the papers.
He made the soccer team.

MODISMOS

Made se usa frecuentemente en modismos. Un modismo es un grupo de palabras que tiene un significado especial. Es muy difícil o a veces imposible de entender este significado con estudiar las palabras separadas. Tiene que aprender de memoria el significado de cada modismo por entero.

EXERCISE 1

Change the following sentences to the past tense.

EJERCICIO 1

Cambie las siguientes oraciones al pretérito.

1. I drink my coffee without sugar.

----

2. We eat all of the cake.

----

3. She makes a dress with that material.

----

4. Gary eats a piece of pie.

----

5. What makes it change color?

----

6. Lupe eats the tortillas.

EXERCISE 2

Fill in the blanks with the words *made, ate,* and *drank.*

EJERCICIO 2

Llene los espacios con las palabras *made, ate,* y *drank.*

1. She _____ all the juice.

2. The company _____ a profit.

3. We _____ all the food on the table.

4. Who _____ this bookcase?

5. The baby _____ the milk.

6. I _____ an appointment to see the dentist.

7. Arturo _____ some chocolate.

8. They _____ supper very late.

9. You _____ a mistake.

10. Sara _____ her coffee slowly.

12. More Irregular Verbs

12. Más Verbos Irregulares

INFINITIVES AND PAST FORMS

to sleep	slept
to wake (up)	woke (up)
to awake	awoke

INFINITIVOS

dormir
despertarse
despertarse

SENTENCES

Repeat with your teacher.

ORACIONES

Repita con su maestro o maestra.

They **awoke** at six.
We **woke** up very early.
He **slept** during the movie.
The sick baby **slept** very little.
What **woke** you up?
I **awoke** because of the noise.
I **slept** for ten hours.
She **woke** up in the middle of the night.
The police siren **awoke** them.

EXERCISE 1

Change these sentences to the past tense.

EJERCICIO 1

Cambie estas oraciones al pretérito.

1. Nicolás wakes up very early.

   ----

2. The cat sleeps in the kitchen.

   ----

3. I awake often during the night.

   ----

4. She sleeps all morning.

   ----

5. I wake up because of a nightmare.

   ----

6. He awakes suddenly.

   ----

7. We sleep on the floor.

----

8. They wake up very late.

----

9. You wake up very easily.

----

10. Laura sleeps for seven hours.

----

11. They sleep in the other room.

----

12. She awakes very slowly.

EXERCISE 2

Write sentences using the past tense of each of the following verbs at least once: *to make, to eat, to drink, to sleep, to wake (up),* and *to awake.*

EJERCICIO 2

Escriba oraciones usando el pretérito de cada uno de los siguientes verbos a lo menos una vez: *to make, to eat, to drink, to sleep, to wake (up),* y *to awake.*

1. --

2. --

3. --

4. --

5. --

6. --

7. --

8. --

13. To Do

INFINITIVE AND PAST FORM

to do   did

USAGE

Did has several uses. It can be used as a complete verb.

> EXAMPLES (EJEMPLOS):
> He did his work.
> They did their laundry.
> I did the dishes.
> She did her homework.
> They did the heavy work.

Did can also be used as a helping verb to give emphasis to a statement.

> EXAMPLES (EJEMPLOS):
> You did drink all the water.
> He did wake me up.
> We did help him.
> I did clean my room.
> They did make it wrong.

Notice that when *did* is used as a helping verb, the main verb is in the basic verb form (the infinitive without the *to*).

EXERCISE

Change the following sentences to give more emphasis. Remember to change the verb to its basic form.

1. I washed my hands.

   ----

2. We rested enough.

   ----

3. I made the table.

   ----

4. You ate too much.

   ----

13. Hacer

INFINITIVO

hacer

USO

Did tiene varios usos. Se puede usar como verbo completo.

Did también se puede usar como verbo ayudante para dar énfasis a una declaración.

Note que cuando *did* se usa como verbo ayudante, el verbo mayor toma la forma básica (el infinitivo sin el *to*).

EJERCICIO

Cambie las siguientes oraciones para dar más énfasis. Recuerde de cambiar el verbo a la forma básica.

14. Negatives

The word *did* is often used in forming negative sentences in the past tense. Notice that since *did* is used as a helping verb, the main verb is in the basic form.

Repeat with your teacher.

> I **did** not **drink** the soda.
> Rolando **did** not **sleep** last night.
> She **did** not **wake** up.
> You **did** not **clean** the floor.

Didn't is a contraction of *did* and *not*. Repeat with your teacher.

> She **did**n't **help** us.
> They **did**n't **rest** at all.
> I **did**n't **eat** the enchiladas.
> Albert **did**n't **make** any noise.
> It **did**n't **dry** very fast.

EXERCISE 1

Change the following sentences to the negative. Use the words *did* and *not*.

1. They cleaned the attic.

   ----

2. You washed your face.

   ----

3. He made an appointment.

   ----

4. Rosa and Antonio drank tea.

   ----

5. She helped us with our spelling.

   ----

6. I ate pie.

   ----

14. Negativos

La palabra *did* se usa frecuentemente para formar oraciones negativas en el pretérito. Note que como *did* es verbo ayudante, el verbo mayor toma la forma básica.

Repita con su maestro o maestra.

Didn't es una contracción de *did* y *not*. Repita con su maestra o maestro.

EJERCICIO 1

Cambie las siguientes oraciones al negativo. Use las palabras *did* y *not*.

7. He slept on the grass.

----

8. We dried the dishes.

EXERCISE 2

Change the following sentences to the negative. Use the contraction *didn't*.

EJERCICIO 2

Cambie las siguientes oraciones al negativo. Use la contracción *didn't*.

1. He helped me with my math.

----

2. They woke up at seven.

----

3. I cooked a large meal.

----

4. We rested after we finished.

----

5. He cleaned his tools.

----

6. Mary washed all of the windows.

VERB CROSSWORD PUZZLE

Fill in the blanks with the correct English verbs in the past tense. Do not write the subject pronouns (he, she, or it).

CRUCIGRAMA DE VERBOS

Llene los espacios con los verbos correctos en inglés en el pretérito. No escriba los pronombres sujetos (he, she, o it).

HORIZONTAL

1. lavó
6. comió
7. limpió
8. descansó
10. secó

VERTICAL

2. ayudó
3. bebió
4. hizo
5. se despertó
9. durmió

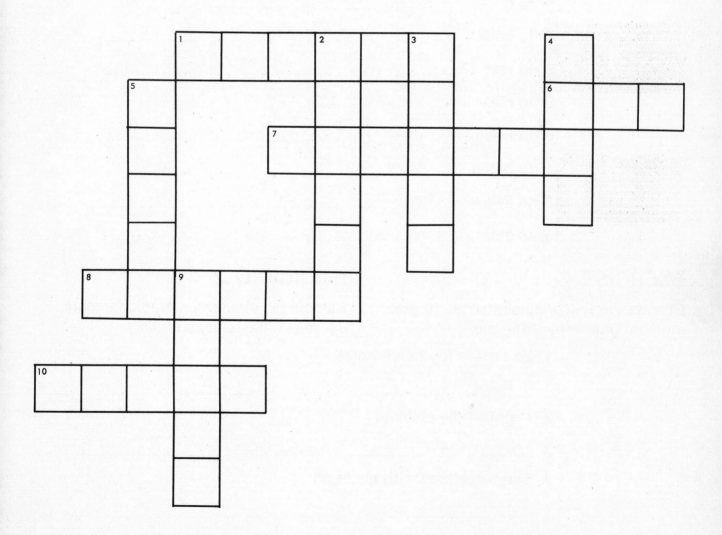

Review of Section II

Repaso de Sección II

EXERCISE 1

Write the past form beside each infinitive. Then write **R** if the verb is regular or **I** if it is irregular.

EJERCICIO 1

Escriba el pretérito al lado de cada infinitivo. Luego escriba **R** si el verbo es regular o **I** si es irregular.

1. to help _____ _____
2. to drink _____ _____
3. to sleep _____ _____
4. to wake (up) _____ _____
5. to make _____ _____
6. to dry _____ _____
7. to cook _____ _____
8. to rest _____ _____
9. to clean _____ _____
10. to wash _____ _____
11. to bathe _____ _____
12. to awake _____ _____
13. to eat _____ _____

EXERCISE 2

Change the following sentences to give more emphasis by using *did*.

EJERCICIO 2

Cambie las siguientes oraciones para dar más énfasis usando *did*.

1. You made too much noise.

   _____

2. I cooked the chicken.

   _____

3. She helped me with my math.

   _____

4. Robert and Larry cleaned their lockers.

----

5. We washed our feet.

----

6. You woke up the baby.

EXERCISE 3

Change the following sentences to the negative by using *didn't*.

EJERCICIO 3

Cambie las siguientes oraciones al negativo usando *didn't*.

1. You cooked the vegetables enough.

----

2. It made much noise.

----

3. I slept well last night.

----

4. She cleaned the inside of her car.

----

5. Ed helped us load the truck.

----

6. We ate at the party.

----

7. Teresa cooked a large meal.

----

8. The sun dried the clothes.

SECTION III
Verbs Dealing with Economics

SECCIÓN III
Verbos sobre la Economía

15. Questions

15. Preguntas

POSITIVE QUESTIONS

The word *did* is often used to form questions in the past tense. In this case, *did* has no Spanish translation. Repeat with your teacher.

PREGUNTAS POSITIVAS

La palabra *did* se usa frecuentemente para formar preguntas en el pretérito. En este caso, *did* no tiene traducción al español. Repita con su maestra o maestro.

Did they **help** carry it?
Did you **sleep** well?
Did Elio **remember** to go?
Did I **wake** you up?
Did Elsa and Luisa **understand** the lesson?
Did Larry **write** that note?
Did we **study** enough?

Notice that these verbs are in the basic form since *did* is used as a helping verb.

Note que estos verbos toman la forma básica porque *did* se usa como verbo ayudante.

NEGATIVE QUESTIONS

The word *didn't* is often used to form negative questions in the past tense. Repeat with your teacher.

PREGUNTAS NEGATIVAS

La palabra *didn't* se usa frecuentemente para formar preguntas negativas en el pretérito. Repita con su maestra o maestro.

Didn't you **know** the answer?
Didn't she **read** the notice?
Didn't he **tell** you about it?
Didn't the teacher **correct** those papers?
Didn't you **study** for the test?
Didn't I **wash** that already?
Didn't they **help** you?

EXERCISE 1

Rewrite the following sentences as positive questions.

EJERCICIO 1

Escriba de nuevo las siguientes oraciones como preguntas positivas.

1. He studied for the exam.

----

2. You did the laundry.

----

3. They repeated the lesson.

----

4. She helped him with his math.

EXERCISE 2

Rewrite the following sentences as negative questions.

EJERCICIO 2

Escriba de nuevo las siguientes oraciones como preguntas negativas.

1. He listened to the song.

----

2. The medicine helped you.

----

3. She cleaned her room.

----

4. They understood the instructions.

----

16. Regular Verbs

16. Verbos Regulares

INFINITIVES AND PAST FORMS

to count	counted
to work	worked
to earn	earned
to owe	owed
to save	saved

INFINITIVOS

contar
trabajar
ganar
deber
guardar

USAGE

Counted is usually used to describe the act of finding a total by numbering.

> EXAMPLE (EJEMPLO):
> They counted the bricks.

Counted on or *counted upon* is used in the sense of depending on someone or something.

> EXAMPLES (EJEMPLOS):
> We counted on clear weather.
> I counted upon his helping me.

USO

Counted se usa usualmente para describir el acto de figurar un total con numerar.

Counted on o *counted upon* se usa en el sentido de depender en alguien o algo.

SENTENCES

Repeat these sentences with your teacher.

ORACIONES

Repita estas oraciones con su maestro o maestra.

> I **worked** hard.
> She **counted** the money carefully.
> Rudy **earned** overtime pay.
> We still **owed** money on our car loan.
> They **saved** their stamps.
> I **saved** my money for a year.
> The motor **worked** perfectly.
> We **counted** on him to remember.
>
> **Did** you **save** your ticket?
> **Did** Marta **work** here before?
> **Did** they **earn** their pay?
> **Did**n't he **count** the figures correctly?

EXERCISE 1

Fill in each blank with the correct form of *to count, to work, to earn,* or *to save* in the past tense.

EJERCICIO 1

Llene cada espacio con la forma correcta de *to count, to work, to earn,* o *to save* en el pretérito.

1. She _____ the number of boxes in the pile.

2. They _____ their money in a big jar.

3. We _____ eight hours a day at the factory.

4. I _____ a good salary.

5. He _____ on me to correct his work.

6. It _____ all right this morning.

EXERCISE 2

Change the first four sentences into positive questions by using *did*. Change sentences 5-8 into negative questions by using *didn't*.

EJERCICIO 2

Cambie las primeras cuatro oraciones a preguntas positivas usando *did*. Cambie oraciones 5-8 a preguntas negativas usando *didn't*.

1. Randy saved his receipts.

   _____

2. You counted the coins twice.

   _____

3. She earned enough money to pay the rent.

   _____

4. They worked on Saturdays.

   _____

5. You saved your pictures.

   _____

6. Charlie worked in an office downtown.

   _____

7. I counted the boxes correctly.

   _____

8. He earned very little.

   _____

17. Answers in the Past Tense

POSITIVE ANSWERS

There are two basic ways to give a positive answer in the past tense to a question beginning with *did* or *didn't*.

You can use *did* in the answer. In this case, the main verb is in the basic form.

EXAMPLES (EJEMPLOS):
Did you study the lesson?
Yes, I did study the lesson.

Did she write this story?
Yes, she did write the story.

Didn't they cook this meal?
Yes, they did cook it.

You can also answer a question without using *did*. In this case, the verb is in the past tense.

EXAMPLES (EJEMPLOS):
Did you speak with your teacher?
Yes, I spoke with my teacher,

Didn't you wake up early this morning?
Yes, I woke up at five.

NEGATIVE ANSWERS

Negative answers usually have the word *didn't* and the verb in basic form.

EXAMPLES (EJEMPLOS):
Did you work there?
No, I didn't work there.

Didn't they count the letters?
No, they didn't count the letters.

EXERCISE 1

Answer these questions in the positive by using *did*.

EXAMPLE (EJEMPLO):
Did she listen to the speech?
Yes, she did listen to the speech.

1. Did you wash the windows?

---

17. Respuestas en el Pretérito

RESPUESTAS POSITIVAS

Hay dos maneras básicas de dar una respuesta positiva a una pregunta comenzando con *did* o *didn't.*

Puede usar *did* en la respuesta. En este caso, el verbo toma la forma básica.

Ud. también puede contestar una pregunta sin usar *did*. En este caso, el verbo está en el pretérito.

RESPUESTAS NEGATIVAS

Respuestas negativas usualmente tienen la palabra *didn't* y el verbo en forma básica.

EJERCICIO 1

Conteste estas preguntas en el positivo usando *did*.

---

2. Did Marcos drink the milk?

----

3. Did he count the pencils?

----

4. Did they work yesterday?

EXERCISE 2

Answer these questions in the positive by using the verb in the past tense.

EXAMPLE (EJEMPLO):
Did they understand the story?
Yes, they understood the story.

EJERCICIO 2

Conteste estas preguntas en el positivo usando el verbo en el pretérito.

1. Did you correct your mistakes?

----

2. Did she read the lesson?

----

3. Did he understand the problem?

EXERCISE 3

Answer these questions in the negative by using *didn't*.

EXAMPLE (EJEMPLO):
Did you forget anything?
No, I didn't forget anything.

EJERCICIO 3

Conteste estas preguntas en el negativo usando *didn't*.

1. Did he translate the poem?

----

2. Did Paul owe any money?

----

3. Did you teach English?

----

18. Short Answers

You can use a short form for positive and negative answers in the past.

EXAMPLES (EJEMPLOS):
Did you make that chair?
Yes, I did.

Did she bathe the baby?
No, she didn't.

Didn't you write him a letter?
Yes, I did.

Didn't they work last Tuesday?
No, they didn't.

EXERCISE 1

Answer the following questions in the positive by using *did*. Then repeat the answers by using the short form.

EXAMPLE (EJEMPLO):
Did you count the change?
Yes, I did count the change.
Yes, I did.

18. Respuestas Cortas

Puede usar una forma corta por respuestas negativas y positivas en el pretérito.

EJERCICIO 1

Conteste las siguientes preguntas en el positivo usando *did*. Luego repita las respuestas usando la forma corta.

1. Did you listen to the news?

----

2. Did they talk to the manager?

----

3. Did she learn German?

----

4. Did it work all right?

EXERCISE 2

Answer the following questions in the negative by using *didn't*. Then repeat the answers by using the short form.

EXAMPLE (EJEMPLO):
Did you save your money?
No, I didn't save my money.
No, I didn't.

EJERCICIO 2

Conteste las siguientes oraciones en el negativo usando *didn't*. Luego repita las respuestas usando la forma corta.

1. Did she eat well?

   ----

2. Did you earn any overtime pay?

   ----

3. Did Felipe rest enough?

   ----

4. Did they help him?

   ----

5. Did he work yesterday?

   ----

6. Did you read the newspaper?

   ----

19. Irregular Verbs

19. Verbos Irregulares

INFINITIVES AND PAST FORMS

INFINITIVOS

to buy	bought
to sell	sold
to pay	paid
to spend	spent

comprar
vender
pagar
gastar

SENTENCES

ORACIONES

Repeat these sentences with your teacher.

Repita estas oraciones con su maestra o maestro.

They **spent** all their money.
He **paid** too much for his car.
Lucy **spent** the extra money.
You **sold** your old car.

Did she **sell** her bicycle?
Yes, she **sold** it.

Did they **buy** a new house?
Yes, they **did buy** one.

Did he **pay** the rent?
No, he **did**n't.

EXERCISE 1

EJERCICIO 1

Change the following sentences to the past tense.

Cambie las siguientes oraciones al pretérito.

1. They buy some ice cream.

   ----

2. She sells her paintings.

   ----

3. Does he spend his money wisely?

   ----

4. She pays her bills.

   ----

5. I sell my books.

   ----

6. Do they pay cash for their clothes?

----

7. He buys some fruit.

EXERCISE 2

Rewrite the following sentences as positive questions.

EJERCICIO 2

Escriba de nuevo las siguientes oraciones como preguntas positivas.

1. She bought a dress.

----

2. They paid off their loan.

----

3. They spent all their money.

----

4. He sold his plants.

EXERCISE 3

Answer the following questions in the positive. Answer with the verb in the past tense.

EXAMPLE (EJEMPLO):
Did she buy any vegetables?
Yes, she bought some vegetables.

EJERCICIO 3

Conteste las siguientes preguntas en el positivo. Conteste con el verbo en el pretérito.

1. Did they sell their ranch?

----

2. Did you pay the phone bill?

----

3. Did the child spend all of her allowance?

----

4. Did he buy a new hat?

----

20. More Irregular Verbs

20. Más Verbos Irregulares

INFINITIVES AND PAST FORMS

to have	had
to keep	kept
to cost	cost

INFINITIVOS

tener
guardar
costar

SENTENCES

Repeat with your teacher.

ORACIONES

Repita con su maestra o maestro.

> She **had** the right answer.
> I **had** a good time at the party.
> He **had** a headache.
> The TV **cost** too much.
> She **kept** all the empty boxes.
>
> **Did** you **keep** the change?
> Yes, I **did**.
>
> **Did** he **have** a good job?
> Yes, he **had** a good job.

Had is often used with an infinitive. In this case, *had* is translated into the past tense of *tener que*.

> EXAMPLES (EJEMPLOS):
> She had to sell her house.
> We had to work on Saturdays.

Had se usa frecuentemente con un infinitivo. En este caso, *had* se traduce al pretérito de *tener que*.

EXERCISE 1

Fill in each blank with the correct form of *to have*, *to keep*, or *to cost* in the past tense.

EJERCICIO 1

Llene cada espacio con la forma correcta de *to have*, *to keep*, o *to cost* en el pretérito.

1. I _____ a bad day at work.

2. Did it _____ very much?

3. I _____ my coat in the other closet.

4. These pants _____ more than the others.

5. Frank and Sally _____ to learn Spanish.

6. He _____ the meat in the refrigerator.

EXERCISE 2

Complete the answers to the following questions. Use *did* or *didn't* and the basic form of the verb.

EXAMPLE (EJEMPLO):
Did you have a sweater on yesterday?
Yes, I did have a sweater on yesterday.

EJERCICIO 2

Complete las respuestas a las siguientes preguntas. Use *did* o *didn't* y la forma básica del verbo.

1. Did you keep the papers?

   No, _____

2. Did she have the newspaper?

   Yes, _____

3. Did they cost very little?

   Yes, _____

4. Did he have a red car?

   No, _____

EXERCISE 3

Complete the answers to the following questions by using the short form.

EXAMPLE (EJEMPLO):
Did it cost twenty dollars?
Yes, it did.

EJERCICIO 3

Complete las respuestas a las siguientes preguntas usando la forma corta.

1. Did Gloria have to correct her work?

   No, _____

2. Did they keep their workbooks?

   Yes, _____

3. Did it cost less than the others?

   Yes, _____

4. Did you keep my picture?

   No, _____

21. Ordinal Numbers

21. Números Ordinales

In *Book 1* we studied numbers such as *one (1)*, *two (2)*, *three (3)*, etc. These are called cardinal numbers.

There are other numbers called ordinal numbers. These are numbers such as *first*, *second*, *third*, etc. Ordinal numbers show position in a series.

Repeat these ordinal numbers with your teacher.

En *Libro 1* estudiamos números como *uno (1)*, *dos (2)*, *tres (3)*, etc. Estos se llaman números cardinales.

Existen otros números llamados números ordinales. Estos son números como *primero(a)*, *segundo(a)*, *tercero(a)*, etc. Números ordinales demuestran posición en una serie.

Repita estos números ordinales con su maestra o maestro.

1st	first	17th	seventeenth
2nd	second	18th	eighteenth
3rd	third	19th	nineteenth
4th	fourth	20th	twentieth
5th	fifth	21st	twenty-first
6th	sixth	22nd	twenty-second
7th	seventh	30th	thirtieth
8th	eighth	40th	fortieth
9th	ninth	50th	fiftieth
10th	tenth	60th	sixtieth
11th	eleventh	70th	seventieth
12th	twelfth	80th	eightieth
13th	thirteenth	90th	ninetieth
14th	fourteenth	100th	one hundredth
15th	fifteenth	101st	one hundred and first
16th	sixteenth	1000th	one thousandth

DICTATION

The teacher will dictate some ordinal numbers in English. Write each number and then the word for the number.

DICTADO

La maestra o el maestro va a dictar unos números ordinales en inglés. Escriba cada número y luego el nombre del número.

EXAMPLE (EJEMPLO):

1st first

1. ---------------- --

2. ---------------- --

3. ---------------- --

4. --------------- --

5. --------------- --

6. --------------- --

7. --------------- --

8. --------------- --

9. --------------- --

10. --------------- --

11. --------------- --

12. --------------- --

13. --------------- --

14. --------------- --

15. --------------- --

16. --------------- --

17. --------------- --

18. --------------- --

19. --------------- --

20. --------------- --

21. --------------- --

22. --------------- --

23. --------------- --

24. --------------- --

25. --------------- --

Review of Section III

EXERCISE 1

Write the past form beside each infinitive. Then write **R** if the verb is regular or **I** if it is irregular.

1. to have
2. to work
3. to buy
4. to sell
5. to pay
6. to cost
7. to earn
8. to spend
9. to owe
10. to keep
11. to save
12. to count

EXERCISE 2

Rewrite the following sentences as positive questions.

1. He sold his refrigerator.

2. Silvia had a large dog.

3. It cost over fifty dollars.

4. He owed you money.

Repaso de Sección III

EJERCICIO 1

Escriba el pretérito al lado de cada infinitivo. Luego escriba **R** si el verbo es regular o **I** si es irregular.

EJERCICIO 2

Escriba de nuevo las siguientes oraciones como preguntas positivas.

EXERCISE 3

Answer the following questions in the positive. Answer with the verb in the past tense.

EXAMPLE (EJEMPLO):
Did the car have a radio?
Yes, the car had a radio.

EJERCICIO 3

Conteste las siguientes preguntas en el positivo. Conteste con el verbo en el pretérito.

1. Did you save money last year?

----

2. Did Harry work very hard?

----

3. Did she keep the pens?

EXERCISE 4

Complete the answers to the following questions. Use *did* or *didn't* and the basic form of the verb.

EJERCICIO 4

Complete las respuestas a las siguientes preguntas. Use *did* o *didn't* y la forma básica del verbo.

1. Did Elena sell her camera?

Yes, --

2. Did Ricardo and María pay their taxes?

Yes, --

3. Did you count the papers on that desk?

No, --

EXERCISE 5

Complete the answers to the following questions by using the short form.

EJERCICIO 5

Complete las respuestas a las siguientes preguntas usando la forma corta.

1. Did they work after five?

Yes, --

2. Did she pay for all of it?

Yes, --

3. Did you keep my records?

No, --

SECTION IV
Verbs of Motion

SECCIÓN IV
Verbos de Movimiento

22. Regular Verbs

22. Verbos Regulares

INFINITIVES AND PAST FORMS

INFINITIVOS

to travel	traveled	viajar
to walk	walked	andar
to return	returned	volver
to arrive	arrived	llegar
to remain	remained	quedarse
to stay	stayed	quedarse

Notice that the *y* in *stay* is not dropped in forming the past tense. This is because there is a vowel before the *y*.

Note que la *y* en *stay* no se elimina en formar el pretérito. Esto es porque hay una vocal antes de la *y*.

SENTENCES
Repeat with your teacher.

ORACIONES
Repita con su maestro o maestra.

> She **remained** at home.
> I **walked** a long way.
> You **arrived** late.
> Gilbert **stayed** after class.
> We **returned** the books to the library.
> They **traveled** to Mexico last year.
>
> **Did** she **walk** to school today?
> No, she **did**n't.
>
> **Did** you **arrive** on time?
> Yes, I **did**.
>
> **Did** you **return** the papers?
> Yes, I **returned** the papers this morning.
>
> **Did**n't you **stay** too long?
> Yes, I **did**.

EXERCISE 1

Write sentences using the past tense of each of the following verbs at least once: *to travel, to walk, to return, to arrive, to remain,* and *to stay.*

EJERCICIO 1

Escriba oraciones usando el pretérito de cada uno de los siguientes verbos a lo menos una vez: *to travel, to walk, to return, to arrive, to remain,* y *to stay.*

1. --
2. --
3. --
4. --
5. --
6. --
7. --
8. --
9. --
10. --

EXERCISE 2

Cross out the incorrect word.

EJERCICIO 2

Tache la palabra incorrecta.

1. Did you (returned, return) those books?
2. Yes, I (returned, return) them.
3. Did he (stay, stayed) for a long time?
4. No, he didn't (stay, stayed) long.
5. Did she (arrive, arrived) on time?
6. Yes, she did (arrived, arrive) on time.

23. The Past Progressive Tense

23. El Imperfecto

We use the past progressive tense to describe an action continuing in the past.

To form the past progressive we use *was* or *were* along with the *ing* form of the verb (the present participle). This tense usually corresponds to the *imperfecto* in Spanish.

I was walking
you were walking
he, she, it was walking
we were walking
you were walking
they were walking

Remember that when a verb ends in *e*, the *e* is dropped before adding *ing*.

> EXAMPLE (EJEMPLO):
> arriv*é* + ing = arriving

Usamos el tiempo *past progressive* para describir una acción continuando en el pasado.

Para formar el *past progressive* usamos *was* o *were* con la forma *ing* del verbo (el gerundio). Este tiempo usualmente corresponde al imperfecto en español.

estaba andando
estabas andando
estaba andando
estábamos andando
estabais andando
estaban andando

Recuerde que cuando un verbo termina en *e*, se elimina la *e* antes de añadir *ing*.

SENTENCES

Here are some sentences in the past progressive. Repeat with your teacher.

ORACIONES

Aquí están unas oraciones en el imperfecto. Repita con su maestra o maestro.

She **was returning** my dictionary.
I **was walking** on the sidewalk.
They **were traveling** on a bus.
The train **was arriving** on time.
The cat **was remaining** in one place.
They **were traveling** to Canada.
You **were returning** the umbrella.
We **were staying** in a hotel.
He **was walking** by himself.
Lupe **was studying** English.
It **was arriving** late.
Ernesto **was sleeping**.
She **was resting**.

EXERCISE 1

Change the following sentences from
the past to the past progressive.

EJERCICIO 1

Cambie las siguientes oraciones del
pretérito al imperfecto.

1. They walked through the corn fields.

   ----

2. He stayed with his uncle.

   ----

3. We traveled very fast.

   ----

4. I returned to my home.

   ----

5. It arrived one day late.

   ----

6. She walked very slowly.

EXERCISE 2

Fill in the blanks with *was* or *were*.

EJERCICIO 2

Llene los espacios con *was* o *were*.

1. She _____ traveling.

2. We _____ arriving.

3. I _____ walking.

4. They _____ returning.

5. It _____ arriving.

6. You _____ staying.

7. He _____ walking.

8. You _____ arriving.

24. More Regular Verbs

INFINITIVES AND PAST FORMS

to use	used
to wait	waited
to change	changed
to exchange	exchanged
to move	moved
to call	called
to visit	visited

USAGE

Changed and *exchanged* mean almost the same thing. However *exchanged* is used only to describe the change of one thing for another.

Called can be used in the sense of shouting or asking somebody to come, or in the sense of using the phone.

EXAMPLES (EJEMPLOS):
He called for help.
She called her children to come.
I called him on the phone.

Called can also be used in the sense of naming someone or something.

EXAMPLE (EJEMPLO):
He called his dog Midas.

SENTENCES

Repeat with your teacher.

Tony **called** his friend.
She **exchanged** the blue dress for the green one.
We **moved** all the tables.
You **changed** the flat tire.
They **waited** patiently.
I **used** my new pen.

Roberto **was calling** his parents.
Mary **was waiting** at the bus stop.
They **were exchanging** notes.
He **was using** the saw.

24. Más Verbos Regulares

INFINITIVOS

usar
esperar
cambiar
cambiar
mover
llamar
visitar

USO

Changed y *exchanged* significan casi la misma cosa. Pero *exchanged* se usa solamente para describir el cambio de una cosa por otra.

Called se puede usar en el sentido de gritar o pedir a alguien que venga, o en el sentido de usar el teléfono.

Called también se puede usar en el sentido de nombrar alguien o algo.

ORACIONES

Repita con su maestro o maestra.

We **were moving** to a new house.
I **was visiting** my relatives.

Did you **call** your office?
No, I **did**n't.

Did she **wait** for a long time?
Yes, she **waited** for an hour.

Didn't he **visit** his sister?
No, he **did**n't.

EXERCISE 1

Fill in each blank with the correct past tense form or the basic form of *to use, to wait, to change, to exchange, to move,* or *to call.*

1. He _____ for me a long time.

2. We _____ the sofa to the corner.

3. Did you _____ my knife to open the box?

4. She _____ you yesterday.

5. I _____ the sweater for a shirt.

6. Mark _____ the channel on the TV.

EXERCISE 2

Fill in the blanks with the correct forms of *to use, to wait, to change, to exchange, to move,* and *to call* in the past progressive.

1. Mike _____ _____ a new hammer.

2. We _____ _____ for the bus.

3. They _____ _____ their clothes.

4. She _____ _____ her pencil for a pen.

5. I _____ _____ by long distance.

6. Francisco and I _____ _____ the boxes.

EJERCICIO 1

Llene cada espacio con la forma correcta en el pretérito o la forma básica de *to use, to wait, to change, to exchange, to move,* o *to call.*

EJERCICIO 2

Llene los espacios con las formas correctas de *to use, to wait, to change, to exchange, to move,* y *to call* en el imperfecto.

25. Negatives in the Past Progressive

25. Negativos en el Imperfecto

To form negative sentences in the past progressive, we use *was not* or *were not* and the present participle.

> EXAMPLES (EJEMPLOS):
> She was not using the typewriter.
> We were not staying at that hotel.
> He was not waiting for us.

Para formar oraciones negativas en el imperfecto, usamos *was not* o *were not* y el gerundio.

You can also use *wasn't* or *weren't* to form negatives in the past progressive.

> EXAMPLES (EJEMPLOS):
> I wasn't staying for the show.
> Graciela wasn't walking to school.
> They weren't traveling by train.
> It wasn't moving at all.
> He wasn't changing the color.
> We weren't arriving on time.

Puede también usar *wasn't* o *weren't* para formar negativos en el imperfecto.

EXERCISE 1

EJERCICIO 1

Change the following sentences to the negative. Use the word *not*.

Cambie las siguientes oraciones al negativo. Use la palabra *not*.

1. Susan and Jennie were traveling very far.

----

2. I was waiting for you.

----

3. You were walking very fast.

----

4. He was returning my scissors.

----

5. They were staying overnight.

----

6. You were using the phone.

----

7. He was moving very slowly.

----

8. We were exchanging gifts.

----

9. Rubén was working on Saturday.

EXERCISE 2

Change the following sentences to the negative. Use the contractions *wasn't* and *weren't*.

EJERCICIO 2

Cambie las siguientes oraciones al negativo. Use las contracciones *wasn't* y *weren't*.

1. You were using the saw correctly.

----

2. The bus was arriving on time.

----

3. They were moving to another city.

----

4. Betty was waiting for a taxi.

----

5. We were traveling by train.

----

6. I was walking to the store.

----

7. Robert was staying at a hotel.

----

8. Manuel and Lupe were exchanging notes.

----

26. Irregular Verbs

26. Verbos Irregulares

INFINITIVES AND PAST FORMS

to drive   drove
to go   went
to come   came
to leave   left
to bring   brought
to take   took

INFINITIVOS

conducir
ir
venir
salir, dejar
traer
tomar, llevar

SENTENCES

Repeat with your teacher.

ORACIONES

Repita con su maestra o maestro.

I **came** to school last year.
You **went** to the doctor.
He **drove** his car to Mexico.
They **took** a trip to Washington.
We **brought** our lunch to work.
She **left** her books at school.

I **was coming** to school to study English.
They **were going** for a ride.
We **were taking** a special trip.
She **was leaving** home.
He **was driving** too fast.
You **were going** to the dentist.

Did you **bring** your lunch?
Yes, I **brought** it.

Did you **go** to the dance?
No, I **did**n't.

EXERCISE 1

Change the following sentences to the past tense.

EJERCICIO 1

Cambie las siguientes oraciones al pretérito.

1. She drives a pickup.

----

2. We go to the movies.

----

3. Albert and Jane come to the party.

56

4. You leave your sweater at my house.

----

5. He takes the medicine.

----

6. I bring an extra pencil to school.

EXERCISE 2

Change the following sentences from the present to the past progressive.

EJERCICIO 2

Cambie las siguientes oraciones del presente al imperfecto.

1. Margarita goes to the bank.

----

2. I take night classes.

----

3. He drives a truck.

----

4. They come home.

----

5. We bring some flowers.

----

6. They leave in the morning.

EXERCISE 3

Cross out the incorrect word or phrase.

EJERCICIO 3

Tache la palabra o frase incorrecta.

1. The students (was, were) taking a test.
2. Did you (brought, bring) the jack?
3. I (went, were going) to the store.
4. Mary and Nancy (was, were) leaving.
5. He (was, were) driving too slowly.
6. Did she (took, take) the packages?

27. Can and To Be Able

Poder

INFINITIVES AND PAST FORMS

INFINITIVOS

can	could
to be able	was or were able

poder
poder

USAGE

USO

Could is usually used as a helping verb. Notice that the main verb is in the basic form.

Usualmente *could* se usa como verbo ayudante. Note que el verbo mayor toma la forma básica.

> EXAMPLES (EJEMPLOS):
> She could drive a truck.
> We could bring our families.
> They could speak English.
> He could understand the words.
> I could walk very fast.
>
> Could he move the heavy crate?
> Yes, he could.

Sometimes *could* is used instead of *can* in the present tense.

A veces *could* se usa en lugar de *can* en el tiempo presente.

> EXAMPLE (EJEMPLO):
> Can you help me now?
> Could you help me now?

Could is also used to express probable action.

Could también se puede usar para expresar acción probable.

> EXAMPLE (EJEMPLO):
> It could rain today.

Was able and *were able* are usually used with infinitives.

Was able y *were able* se usan usualmente con infinitivos.

> EXAMPLES (EJEMPLOS):
> I was able to go to work.
> She was able to travel after a week.
> We were able to return.
> You were able to move.
> They were able to stay longer.

EXERCISE 1

EJERCICIO 1

Write sentences using *could*.

Escriba oraciones usando *could*.

1. _____

2. _____

3. _____

4. _____

5. _____

6. _____

7. _____

8. _____

EXERCISE 2

Write sentences using *was able*.

EJERCICIO 2

Escriba oraciones usando *was able*.

1. _____

2. _____

3. _____

4. _____

5. _____

6. _____

7. _____

8. _____

EXERCISE 3

Write sentences using *were able*.

EJERCICIO 3

Escriba oraciones usando *were able*.

1. _____

2. _____

3. _____

4. _____

5. _____

6. _____

7. _____

8. _____

28. Negative Sentences with Can and To Be Able

28. Oraciones Negativas con Poder

Here are some negative sentences with *could, was able,* and *were able.*

EXAMPLES (EJEMPLOS):
He could not move very much.
We could not stay very long.
She could not return.

We were not able to call.
Mary was not able to go.
They were not able to use the blackboard.

You can also use the contractions *wasn't, weren't,* and *couldn't* to form the negative. *Couldn't* is the contraction of *could* and *not.*

EXAMPLES (EJEMPLOS):
Elsa and César couldn't leave yesterday.
I couldn't wait for too long.
He couldn't take the medicine.

We weren't able to visit her.
Joe wasn't able to walk for a while.
You weren't able to exchange the coat for another.

Aquí están unas oraciones negativas con *could, was able,* y *were able.*

Ud. también puede usar las contracciones *wasn't, weren't,* y *couldn't* para formar el negativo. *Couldn't* es la contracción de *could* y *not.*

EXERCISE 1

Change these sentences to the negative by using the word *not.*

EXAMPLE (EJEMPLO):
He could drive a car.
He could not drive a car.

EJERCICIO 1

Cambie estas oraciones al negativo usando la palabra *not.*

1. She was able to travel often.

----

2. We could use the elevator.

----

3. I could change it.

----

4. It could move by itself.

EXERCISE 2

Change each sentence to the negative by using the contraction *wasn't, weren't,* or *couldn't*.

EJERCICIO 2

Cambie cada oración al negativo usando la contracción *wasn't, weren't,* o *couldn't*.

1. We could go to the show.

----

2. Antonio was able to use the machine.

----

3. They were able to bring their notes.

----

4. I could drive the truck.

----

5. I was able to stay there for an hour.

----

6. You were able to move the desk.

CONTRACTION WHEEL

Here is a contraction wheel with some of the contractions used in the past and past progressive tenses.

RUEDA DE CONTRACCIONES

Aquí está una rueda de contracciones con unas de las contracciones que se usan en el pretérito y imperfecto.

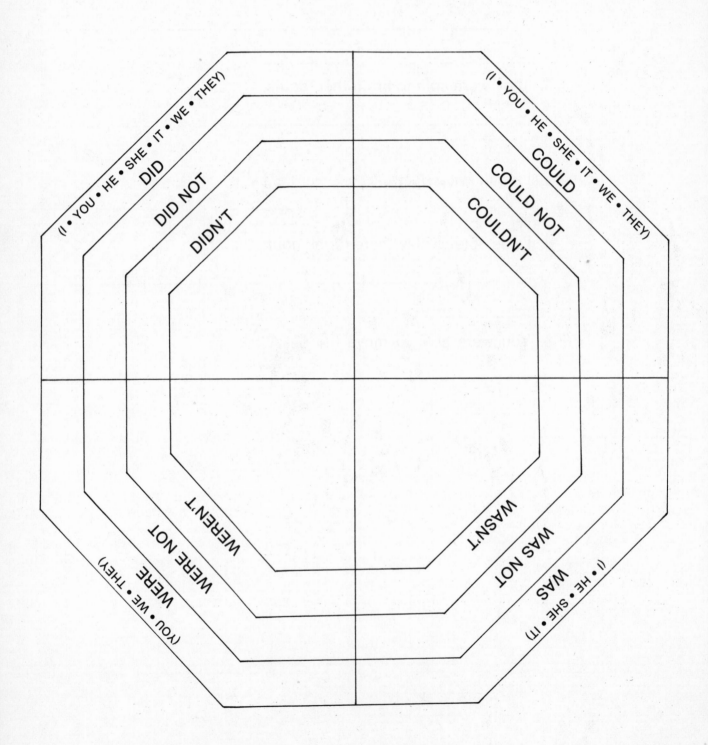

EXERCISE

Can you fill in the blanks with the correct words without looking at the previous page?

EJERCICIO

¿Puede Ud. llenar los espacios con las palabras correctas sin mirar a la página anterior?

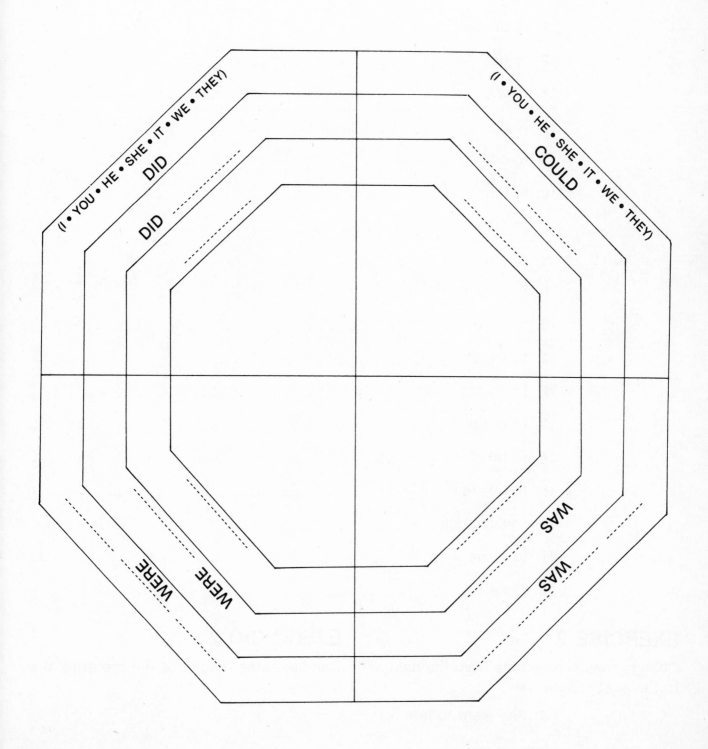

Review of Section IV

EXERCISE 1

Write the past form beside each infinitive. Then write **R** if the verb is regular or **I** if it is irregular.

Repaso de Sección IV

EJERCICIO 1

Escriba el pretérito al lado de cada infinitivo. Luego escriba **R** si el verbo es regular o **I** si es irregular.

1. to drive ------------------------------ ------
2. to use ------------------------------ ------
3. to walk ------------------------------ ------
4. to go ------------------------------ ------
5. to come ------------------------------ ------
6. to leave ------------------------------ ------
7. to arrive ------------------------------ ------
8. to stay ------------------------------ ------
9. to return ------------------------------ ------
10. to visit ------------------------------ ------
11. to travel ------------------------------ ------
12. to wait ------------------------------ ------
13. to bring ------------------------------ ------
14. to take ------------------------------ ------
15. to change ------------------------------ ------
16. to exchange ------------------------------ ------
17. to move ------------------------------ ------
18. to call ------------------------------ ------

EXERCISE 2

Change these sentences from the past to the past progressive.

1. She went to lunch.

EJERCICIO 2

Cambie estas oraciones del pretérito al imperfecto.

----

2. They returned by car.

----

3. He changed the questions.

----

4. The teacher brought a cake to the students.

----

5. They took notes in class.

EXERCISE 3

Cross out the incorrect word.

EJERCICIO 3

Tache la palabra incorrecta.

1. Frank and Elaine (were, was) traveling by airplane.
2. Did you (go, went) to the bullfight?
3. They were (leaving, left) at three.
4. I (was, were) using the dictionary.
5. Did she (visited, visit) her aunt?
6. Where did you (took, take) them?
7. Susan and Linda were (arrived, arriving) in the morning.
8. He could not (drive, drove) a car with a standard transmission.

EXERCISE 4

Rewrite the following sentences by using contractions.

EJERCICIO 4

Escriba de nuevo las siguientes oraciones usando contracciones.

1. He was not able to return for a week.

----

2. They were not able to use the tools.

----

3. Julia could not come to class.

----

4. I was not able to leave on time.

----

5. They could not remain there any longer.

SECTION V
Problem Verbs

29. To Give, To Get, and To Receive

INFINITIVES AND PAST FORMS

to give	gave
to get	got
to receive	received

Study the verbs above. Which one is regular, and which are irregular?

SENTENCES
Repeat with your teacher.

I **gave** her a toy.
She **got** a raise from her boss.
We **received** a package in the mail.
You **got** a speeding ticket.
Carlos **received** a check.
We **could**n't **get** it in time.

They **were getting** sick.
He **was getting** tired.
She **was receiving** a pension.
Mike **was giving** him a gift.
We **were getting** new clothes.

Did you **get** my message?
Yes, I **got** it this morning.

Did they **receive** any mail?
Yes, they **did**.

Got, was getting, and *were getting* are sometimes used in idioms. Often they are followed by a preposition or an adverb.

EXAMPLES (EJEMPLOS):
We were getting along fine.
She got her way.
The noise was getting on my nerves.

SECCIÓN V
Verbos de Problemas

29. Dar, Conseguir, y Recibir

INFINITIVOS

dar
conseguir
recibir

Estudie los verbos de arriba. ¿Cual es regular y cuales son irregulares?

ORACIONES
Repita con su maestra o maestro.

Got, was getting, y *were getting* se usan a veces en modismos. Frecuentemente toman una preposición o un adverbio.

EXERCISE 1

Change these sentences to the past tense.

EJERCICIO 1

Cambie estas oraciones al pretérito.

1. The teacher gives a party for the class.

   ----

2. We receive good news.

   ----

3. They get a new car.

   ----

4. She receives much praise for her work.

   ----

5. I give him my pencil.

   ----

6. The car gets good mileage.

EXERCISE 2

Rewrite these sentences as questions.

EJERCICIO 2

Escriba de nuevo estas oraciones como preguntas.

1. You got the paper today.

   ----

2. She received a phone call.

   ----

3. He gave them the money.

   ----

4. She got the right answer.

   ----

30. To Thank and To Think

30. Agradecer y Pensar

INFINITIVES AND PAST FORMS

to thank   thanked
to think   thought

INFINITIVOS

agradecer
pensar

SENTENCES

Study the verbs above. Pronounce the verbs carefully. Then repeat the sentences below with your teacher.

ORACIONES

Estudie los verbos de arriba. Pronuncie los verbos cuidadosamente. Luego repita las oraciones con su maestra o maestro.

I **thanked** the students for their help.
I **thought** about the problem.
You **were thanking** her for the present.
You **were thinking** about the test.
María **was thanking** the teacher.
Edward **was thinking** hard.
We **thanked** our host for the dinner.
We **thought** about our new jobs.

Did the children **thank** the lady?
Yes, they **did**.

Did the students **think** about their grades?
Yes, they **thought** about them.

Did you **think** about a place for the picnic?
No, I **did**n't.

EXERCISE

Cross out the incorrect word.

EJERCICIO

Tache la palabra incorrecta.

1. We were (thought, thinking) about leaving.
2. Did you (thanked, thank) him for his help?
3. What did he (think, thought) about it?
4. Gilbert and I (were, was) thinking of going home.
5. We (thanking, thanked) them for their consideration.
6. I (thinking, thought) it was a good idea.
7. We (were, was) thinking of returning.
8. She (thinking, thought) the answer was wrong.
9. He didn't (think, thought) it was late.
10. You (were, was) thanking them for their assistance.

31. To Look and To See

31. Mirar y Ver

INFINITIVES AND PAST FORMS

INFINITIVOS

to look   looked
to see   saw

mirar
ver

SENTENCES

ORACIONES

Repeat with your teacher.

Repita con su maestro o maestra.

I **saw** a good movie last night.
We **looked** at the ships.
They **looked** at the painting.
Kevin **was looking** into the box.
You **saw** that movie.
I **was seeing** spots before my eyes.
She **could**n't **see** anything.

Did you **see** the play?
Yes, I **saw** it Sunday.

Looked for, was looking for, and *were looking for* are used in the sense of searching for something (buscar).

Looked for, was looking for, y *were looking for* se usan en el sentido de buscar por algo.

EXAMPLES (EJEMPLOS):
We were looking for her lost purse.
He looked for his wallet.

Looked is sometimes used in the sense of to appear or to seem.

Looked se usa a veces en el sentido de parecer.

EXAMPLES (EJEMPLOS):
The town looked deserted.
He looked like his father.
She looked tired.

EXERCISE 1

EJERCICIO 1

Write sentences using the past tense of *to see.*

Escriba oraciones usando el pretérito de *to see.*

1. _____

2. _____

3. _____

4. _____

5. _____

69

6. _____

7. _____

8. _____

EXERCISE 2

Write sentences using the past progressive of *to look*.

EJERCICIO 2

Escriba oraciones usando el imperfecto de *to look*.

1. _____

2. _____

3. _____

4. _____

5. _____

6. _____

7. _____

8. _____

EXERCISE 3

Write sentences using the past progressive of *to look (for)*.

EJERCICIO 3

Escriba oraciones usando el imperfecto de *to look (for)*.

1. _____

2. _____

3. _____

4. _____

5. _____

6. _____

7. _____

8. _____

32. To Break, To Tear, To Repair, and To Fix

32. Quebrar, Romper, Reparar, y Arreglar

INFINITIVES AND PAST FORMS

to break	broke
to tear	tore
to repair	repaired
to fix	fixed

INFINITIVOS

quebrar
romper
reparar
arreglar

USAGE

Tore is used to describe an action on objects such as paper, books, or clothing. *Broke* is used to describe an action on objects such as toys, machines, dishes, or windows.

USO

Tore se usa para describir una acción en objetos como papel, libros, o ropa. *Broke* se usa para describir una acción en objetos como jugetes, máquinas, trastes, o ventanas.

SENTENCES

Repeat these sentences with your teacher.

ORACIONES

Repita estas oraciones con su maestro o maestra.

Mario **broke** his leg.
The car **broke** down.
She **tore** her sweater.
They **were tearing** the papers into little pieces.
You **repaired** the broken steps.
He **was repairing** the fence.
Teresa **fixed** the washing machine.
I **fixed** the leaky faucet.

Did they **repair** the motor?
Yes, they **did**.

Did he **break** the window?
Yes, he **broke** it.

EXERCISE 1

Fill in the blanks with the correct words.

EJERCICIO 1

Llene los espacios con las palabras correctas.

1. He _____ his shirt.
   rompió

2. How did you _____ it?
   quebró

3. The dog _____ up the newspaper.
   rompió

4. She _____ _____ the machine.
   estaba   reparando

5. Why did they _____ those windows?
   quebraron

6. He _____ _____ the material with his
   estaba   rompiendo
   teeth.

7. She _____ _____ the flat tire.
   estaba   arreglando

8. When did they _____ the car?
   repararon

9. I _____ the lamp.
   arreglé

10. He _____ his watch.
    quebró

EXERCISE 2

Cross out the incorrect word.

1. We were (tearing, tore) the material.
2. Did you (broke, break) this?
3. Yes, I did (broke, break) it.
4. She was (fixed, fixing) the table.
5. Michael and I (was, were) repairing our bicycles.
6. Frank (tore, tearing) his sweater.
7. The horse (breaking, broke) a bone in her leg.
8. They (tore, tearing) the magazine.
9. Did they (repairing, repair) the sofa?
10. You (fixed, fixing) a very good meal.

EJERCICIO 2

Tache la palabra incorrecta.

33. Questions in the Past Progressive

33. Preguntas en el Imperfecto

Here are some questions and answers in the past progressive. Notice that some of the answers are in short form. Repeat with your teacher.

Aquí están unas preguntas y respuestas en el imperfecto. Note que unas de las respuestas están en forma corta. Repita con su maestra o maestro.

> **Were** you **fixing** the roof?
> Yes, I **was fixing** it.
>
> **Was** she **looking** for the matches?
> Yes, she **was looking** for them.
>
> **Were** they **receiving** any help?
> No, they **were**n't **receiving** any help.
>
> **Was** he **thinking** about the test?
> No, he **was**n't **thinking** about the test.
>
> **Was** it **getting** dark outside?
> Yes, it **was**.
>
> **Were** they **looking** at the words on the blackboard?
> No, they **were**n't.
>
> **Were** you **giving** them the answers?
> Yes, I **was**.
>
> **Were** they **repairing** the old furniture?
> Yes, they **were**.

You can also use *wasn't* or *weren't* to form negative questions in the past progressive.

También puede usar *wasn't* o *weren't* para formar preguntas negativas en el imperfecto.

EXAMPLES (EJEMPLOS):
Weren't you receiving your checks through the mail?
Yes, I was.

Wasn't he looking at the road?
No, he wasn't.

EXERCISE 1

EJERCICIO 1

Rewrite the following sentences as questions in the past progressive.

Escriba de nuevo las siguientes oraciones como preguntas en el imperfecto.

1. Marta was getting the meat for the picnic.

2. They were thinking about the answer to the question.

----

3. He was fixing the ladder.

----

4. You were looking for the pencil sharpener.

----

5. He was giving the children candy.

----

6. Mark and Robert were tearing their old clothes.

EXERCISE 2

Complete the answers to the following questions by using the short form.

EJERCICIO 2

Complete las respuestas a las siguientes preguntas usando la forma corta.

1. Did she break this?

   No, ---

2. Was he looking at the signs?

   Yes, --

3. Was it getting cold?

   No, ---

4. Did you see that movie?

   Yes, --

5. Were they receiving any help from the lawyer?

   Yes, --

6. Were you thinking of going to Mexico?

   Yes, --

34. To Sit, To Set, To Put, and To Place

34. Sentarse y Poner

INFINITIVES AND PAST FORMS

to sit	sat
to set	set
to put	put
to place	placed

INFINITIVOS

sentarse
poner
poner
poner

USAGE

Set has many uses. It can be used in the sense of putting something in its place.

> EXAMPLE (EJEMPLO):
> We set our books on the table.

Set can also be used to describe the act of arranging or adjusting something.

> EXAMPLES (EJEMPLOS):
> He set the alarm clock.
> They set a trap for the coyotes.

Set can also be used to describe the act of establishing a date, a price, a rule, an example, or a limit.

> EXAMPLES (EJEMPLOS):
> They set a date for the party.
> He set the price at twenty dollars.
> They set many new rules.
> They set a good example for their children.
> The teacher set a time limit for the test.

Put on, was putting on, and *were putting on* are usually used in the sense of dressing oneself with something.

> EXAMPLES (EJEMPLOS):
> They were putting on their coats.
> She put on her hat.

USO

Set tiene muchos usos. Se puede usar en el sentido de poner algo en su lugar.

Set también se puede usar para describir el acto de arreglar o ajustar algo.

Set también se puede usar para describir el acto de establecer un tiempo, un precio, una regla, un ejemplo, o un limite.

Put on, was putting on, y *were putting on* se usan usualmente en el sentido de vestirse o ponerse algo.

SENTENCES

Repeat with your teacher.

ORACIONES

Repita con su maestro o maestra.

> I **sat** on the chair.
> She **placed** the napkins on the table.
> Steve **put** the hammer in the drawer.

We **were putting** the groceries away.
You **were**n't **sitting** up straight.
I **was setting** the table.
We **were sitting** on the porch.

Where **did** you **put** the pliers?
I **put** them in that cabinet.

Did he **set** a new price?
Yes, he **did**.

Were they **sitting** on the benches?
Yes, they **were**.

Was he **putting** on his gloves?
No, he **wasn**'t.

Were you **setting** the bait on the trap?
No, I **was**n't.

EXERCISE

Cross out the incorrect word or phrase.

EJERCICIO

Tache la palabra o frase incorrecta.

1. We (set, setting) a date for the fiesta.
2. Did you (put, putting) the ruler here?
3. Where did he (place, placed) the tape?
4. (Were, Was) they (sitting, sat) on the folding chairs?
5. Why did you (sit, sat) down there?
6. Lucy (set, sat) the flowers in a vase.
7. Were they (putting on, put on) their shoes?
8. Did we (sit, sat) in the wrong place?
9. How did you (set, setting) the alarm in the clock?
10. Alberto (placed, place) his tools in the toolbox.
11. How did you (put, putting) the tape on?
12. They (were, was) sitting at the end of the table.
13. She (set, sat) down to rest.
14. Did I (put, put on) the wrong sweater?
15. He (set, sat) the clock back one hour.
16. We (were, was) putting on our coats.

35. To Lay and To Lie

35. Poner, Acostarse, y Mentir

INFINITIVES AND PAST FORMS

to lay	laid	(was, were) laying
to lie	lay	(was, were) lying
to lie	lied	(was, were) lying

INFINITIVOS

poner
acostarse
mentir

USAGE

Notice that the past tense of *to lie (lay)* is the same as the present tense of *to lay.* This often causes confusion.

Lay, laid, was laying, and *were laying* are used in situations in which an object is required.

> EXAMPLES (EJEMPLOS):
> He laid the package on the desk.
> We were laying the boxes in the corner.

Lie, lay, was lying, and *were lying* are used in situations in which there is no object.

> EXAMPLES (EJEMPLOS):
> The books were lying on the floor.
> He lay on a cot.

Note that *to lie* can also be used in the sense of saying something that is not true (*mentir*). In this case, the verb is regular.

> EXAMPLES (EJEMPLOS):
> He lied about his age.
> You were lying to us.

USO

Note que el pretérito de *to lie (lay)* es igual al presente de *to lay.* Esto frecuentemente causa confusión.

Lay, laid, was laying, y *were laying* se usan en situaciones donde se requiere un objeto.

Lie, lay, was lying, y *were lying* se usan en situaciones donde no hay objeto.

Note que *to lie* también se puede usar en el sentido de decir algo que no es verdad (*mentir*). En este caso, el verbo es regular.

SENTENCES

Repeat these sentences with your teacher.

ORACIONES

Repita estas oraciones con su maestra o maestro.

She **laid** the tablecloth on the table.
You **lay** down to rest an hour ago.
I **lied** about my qualifications.
We **laid** our tools on the workbench.
They **were laying** tile.
We never **lied** about anything.

Did she **lay** the hammer on the desk?
Yes, she **laid** it on the desk.

Did they **lie** down on the grass?
Yes, they **lay** on the grass to rest.

Was he **lying** about the money he got?
Yes, he **was lying**.

EXERCISE 1

Fill in each blank with *laid, lay,* or *lied*.

1. Margie _____ her purse on the couch.

2. He _____ about how fast he was driving.

3. They _____ their coats on the bed.

4. The dog _____ under the tree.

EXERCISE 2

Fill in the blanks with *was laying, were laying, was lying,* or *were lying*.

1. He _____ _____ on the sleeping bag.

2. We _____ _____ the logs by the cabin.

3. You _____ _____ about where you went.

4. She _____ _____ the bags of groceries on the table.

5. It _____ _____ on the floor.

6. They _____ _____ the posts on the ground.

EJERCICIO 1

Llene cada espacio con *laid, lay,* o *lied*.

EJERCICIO 2

Llene los espacios con *was laying, were laying, was lying,* o *were lying*.

36. To Let and To Try

INFINITIVES AND PAST FORMS

to let   let
to try   tried

The present participle of *to let* has two *t*'s (*letting*).

SENTENCES

Repeat with your teacher.

The parents **let** their children go to the movies.
We **let** the cat in.
He **let** us get our books.
She **was trying** to speak English.
He **tried** to learn Spanish.
They **were trying** to open the door.

Did the teacher **let** the students use their notebooks?
Yes, the teacher **did**.

Were you **trying** to call him?
No, I **was**n't.

Tried on, was trying on, and *were trying on* are used in the sense of testing something, such as a garment, to see if it fits.

EXAMPLES (EJEMPLOS):
He tried on new shoes.
They were trying on the raincoats.

Tried is sometimes used with *ing* words. In such sentences, the *ing* words are not considered part of the verb.

EXAMPLE (EJEMPLO):
He tried skating last winter.

EXERCISE 1

Write sentences using the past or past progressive of *to let*.

36. Dejar y Tratar

INFINITIVOS

dejar
tratar

El gerundio de *to let* tiene dos *t*'s (*letting*).

ORACIONES

Repita con su maestra o maestro.

Tried on, was trying on, y *were trying on* se usan en el sentido de probar algo, como ropa, para ver si queda bien.

Tried se usa a veces con palabras que terminan con *ing*. En tales oraciones, las palabras con *ing* no se consideran parte del verbo.

EJERCICIO 1

Escriba oraciones usando el pretérito o imperfecto de *to let*.

1. --

2. --

3. --

4. --

5. --

6. --

EXERCISE 2

Write sentences using the past or past progressive of *to try*.

EJERCICIO 2

Escriba oraciones usando el pretérito o imperfecto de *to try*.

1. --

2. --

3. --

4. --

5. --

6. --

EXERCISE 3

Write sentences using the past or past progressive of *to try (on)*.

EJERCICIO 3

Escriba oraciones usando el pretérito o imperfecto de *to try (on)*.

1. --

2. --

3. --

4. --

5. --

6. --

VERB CROSSWORD PUZZLE

Fill in the blanks with the correct words in English. Some are *ing* words and others are verbs in the past tense. Do not write the subject pronouns (he, she, or it).

CRUCIGRAMA DE VERBOS

Llene los espacios con las palabras correctas en inglés. Unas son palabras con *ing* y otras son verbos en el pretérito. No escriba los pronombres sujetos (he, she, o it).

HORIZONTAL

2. dio
4. dejó
6. agradeció
7. trató

VERTICAL

1. recibiendo
2. consiguió
3. miró
4. puso

5. pensando
7. rompió

Review of Section V

Repaso de Sección V

EXERCISE 1

Write the past form beside each infinitive. Then write **R** if the verb is regular or **I** if it is irregular.

EJERCICIO 1

Escriba el pretérito al lado de cada infinitivo. Luego escriba **R** si el verbo es regular o **I** si es irregular.

1. to repair
2. to receive
3. to try
4. to lay
5. to get
6. to break
7. to see
8. to fix
9. to thank
10. to give
11. to place
12. to think
13. to sit
14. to lie
15. to lie (mentir)
16. to set
17. to tear
18. to look

EXERCISE 2

Rewrite the following sentences as questions.

EJERCICIO 2

Escriba de nuevo las siguientes oraciones como preguntas.

1. She was looking at the paintings.

2. They were putting on their boots.

----

3. You were trying to watch television.

----

4. He was lying on the floor.

----

5. They were putting the pieces together.

----

6. Emilio was fixing his motorcycle.

----

7. You were thinking about leaving.

----

8. Nancy and Dorothy were sitting on the park bench.

EXERCISE 3

Complete the answers to these
questions by using the short form.

EJERCICIO 3

Complete las respuestas a estas
preguntas usando la forma corta.

1. Were you looking for the newspaper?

   Yes, ----

2. Did you see my glasses?

   No, ----

3. Were they trying to help you?

   Yes, ----

4. Did you get my message?

   Yes, ----

5. Did he thank them?

   No, ----

6. Was he receiving much mail?

   Yes, ----

SECTION VI
Verbs with Opposite Meanings

37. To Open and To Close

INFINITIVES AND PAST FORMS

to open   opened
to close   closed

SENTENCES

Repeat these sentences with your teacher.

Harry **was opening** the gates.
She **opened** the jar.
They **opened** the windows.
Celia **did**n't **close** the door.
You **were opening** the wrong box.

Did you **open** your gifts?
Yes, I **opened** them this morning.

Were they **closing** the store?
Yes, they **were**.

Could he **open** it?
No, he **could**n't.

EXERCISE 1

In the space beside each group of words, write the letter of the Spanish translation.

1. she opened   ....

2. he was closing   ....

3. she could open   ....

4. he didn't open   ....

5. she was opening ....

SECCIÓN VI
Verbos con Significados Opuestos

37. Abrir y Cerrar

INFINITIVOS

abrir
cerrar

ORACIONES

Repita estas oraciones con su maestro o maestra.

EJERCICIO 1

En el espacio al lado de cada grupo de palabras, escriba la letra de la traducción al español.

a. él no abrió

b. ella abrió

c. ella estaba abriendo

d. él estaba cerrando

e. ella pudo abrir

EXERCISE 2

Change the following sentences to questions.

EJERCICIO 2

Cambie las siguientes oraciones a preguntas.

1. She opened a savings account at the bank.

----

2. He closed his eyes.

----

3. You closed the back door.

----

4. They opened their books to the correct page.

EXERCISE 3

Write sentences using the past or past progressive of *to open*.

EJERCICIO 3

Escriba oraciones usando el pretérito o imperfecto de *to open*.

1. --
2. --
3. --
4. --

EXERCISE 4

Write sentences using the past or past progressive of *to close*.

EJERCICIO 4

Escriba oraciones usando el pretérito o imperfecto de *to close*.

1. --
2. --
3. --
4. --

38. To Live and To Die

38. Vivir y Morir

INFINITIVES AND PAST FORMS

INFINITIVOS

to live   lived
to die   died

vivir
morir

SENTENCES

Repeat with your teacher.

ORACIONES

Repita con su maestra o maestro.

Carlos **lived** in Mexico last year.
I **lived** on a ranch for four years.
He **died** last week.
He **did**n't **die** of cancer.
They **were living** in a very large house.
I **was living** in Canada last summer.

Were they **living** in an apartment?
Yes, they **lived** in an apartment.

Did the fire **die** out?
Yes, it **did**.

Did you ever **live** on Pecan Street?
No, I **did**n't.

EXERCISE

Cross out the incorrect word.

EJERCICIO

Tache la palabra incorrecta.

1. We (was, were) living in a migrant camp.
2. The cat didn't (died, die).
3. He (died, dying) of a heart attack.
4. Did they (live, lived) by the ocean?
5. Where were they (lived, living)?
6. We (living, lived) on the other side of town.
7. When did she (died, die)?
8. They (lived, living) in a very nice house.

39. To Ask and To Answer

39. Preguntar y Contestar

INFINITIVES AND PAST FORMS

INFINITIVOS

to ask   asked
to answer   answered

preguntar
contestar

SENTENCES

ORACIONES

Repeat these sentences with your teacher.

Repita estas oraciones con su maestro o maestra.

She **answered** the phone.
The students **answered** the questions correctly.
Jorge **asked** many questions in class.
We **were asking** for help.
She **did**n't **answer** the second question.
Why **did**n't you **answer** that question?

Did they **ask** you to stay?
Yes, they **did**.

Was he **asking** too many questions?
No, he **was**n't.

Didn't you **ask** him how to do it?
No, I **did**n't.

EXERCISE

EJERCICIO

Rewrite these sentences as questions.

Escriba de nuevo estas oraciones como preguntas.

1. Juanita answered the letter.

----

2. He asked for another serving of food.

----

3. You answered all the questions on the test.

----

4. They were asking for directions.

----

5. She asked where the restaurant was.

----

40. The Imperative

We use the imperative when we give commands. Commands are easy to learn in English. Use the basic form of the verb (the infinitive without the *to*). You usually do not need the subject pronoun *you*.

EXAMPLES (EJEMPLOS):
Open the door.
Please open the door.
You open the door now!
You close the door.
Close the door, please.

Notice that we often use the word *please* for politeness.

We use the words *do not* or *don't* and the basic form of the verb to give negative commands.

EXAMPLES (EJEMPLOS):
Do not answer the phone.
Don't ask any more questions.

We use commands every day. Many of the instructions in this book are in the imperative. Look through the pages in your book. Notice the verbs we use as commands.

SENTENCES

The following sentences are in the imperative. Repeat with your teacher.

40. El Imperativo

Usamos el imperativo cuando damos mandamientos. Es muy fácil aprender mandamientos en inglés. Use la forma básica del verbo (el infinitivo sin el *to*). Usualmente no necesita el pronombre *you*.

Note que frecuentemente se usa la palabra *please* por cortesía.

Usamos las palabras *do not* o *don't* y la forma básica del verbo para dar mandamientos negativos.

Usamos mandamientos cada día. Muchas de las instrucciones en este libro están en el imperativo. Fíjese en las páginas de su libro. Note los verbos que usamos como mandamientos.

ORACIONES

Las siguientes oraciones están en el imperativo. Repita con su maestro o maestra.

Please **open** your book.
Ask me a question.
Answer the question, please.
Please **close** the window.
Don't **put** those books over there.
Please **answer** the phone.
Sit over there.
Please **give** me the book.
Please **do** not **lay** your coats on the bed.

EXERCISE 1

Write *command* in the space if the sentence is a command. Write *statement* if the sentence is a statement. Write *question* if the sentence is a question.

EXAMPLE (EJEMPLO):

He opened the door. *statement*

1. Put the dishes away. ------------------------------------
2. Did you see the ball game? ------------------------------------
3. Please answer the phone. ------------------------------------
4. Mary closed the curtains. ------------------------------------
5. Give him the books, please. ------------------------------------
6. Were they going to the dance? ------------------------------------
7. We lived in an old house. ------------------------------------
8. You fixed it. ------------------------------------

EJERCICIO 1

Escriba *command* en el espacio si la oración es un mandamiento. Escriba *statement* si la oración es una declaración. Escriba *question* si la oración es una pregunta.

EXERCISE 2

Write sentences using commands. Use the words *open*, *close*, *ask*, and *answer*.

1. ------------------------------------
2. ------------------------------------
3. ------------------------------------
4. ------------------------------------
5. ------------------------------------
6. ------------------------------------

EJERCICIO 2

Escriba oraciones usando mandamientos. Use las palabras *open*, *close*, *ask*, y *answer*.

41. To Lose and To Find

41. Perder y Encontrar

INFINITIVES AND PAST FORMS

INFINITIVOS

to lose   lost
to find   found

perder
encontrar

SENTENCES

Repeat with your teacher.

ORACIONES

Repita con su maestra o maestro.

Rubén **found** a nickel.
I **lost** my shoes.
She **found** your notebook.
He **could**n't **find** the word in the dictionary.
They **were losing** the game.
He **found** a hat in the street.

What **did** the students **lose**?
They **lost** their notebooks.

Did you **find** your wallet?
Yes, I **did**.

Did you **lose** your keys again?
No, I **did**n't.

Where **did** you **find** my notebook?
I **found** it at the library.

EXERCISE 1

In the space beside each group of words, write the letter of the Spanish translation.

EJERCICIO 1

En el espacio al lado de cada grupo de palabras, escriba la letra de la traducción al español.

1. she found

2. He was losing.

3. she couldn't find

4. He lost.

5. he wasn't able to find

6. She lost.

------   a. Ella perdió.

------   b. ella no pudo encontrar

------   c. Él estaba perdiendo.

------   d. ella encontró

------   e. él no pudo encontrar

------   f. Él perdió.

EXERCISE 2

Write questions and answers using forms of *to find* in the past tense.

1. ---
   ----
2. ---
   ----
3. ---
   ----
4. ---
   ----
5. ---

EJERCICIO 2

Escriba preguntas y respuestas usando formas de *to find* en el pretérito.

EXERCISE 3

Write questions and answers using forms of *to lose* in the past tense.

1. ---
   ----
2. ---
   ----
3. ---
   ----
4. ---
   ----
5. ---

EJERCICIO 3

Escriba preguntas y respuestas usando formas de *to lose* en el pretérito.

42. To Begin, To Continue, To End, and To Finish

42. Comenzar, Continuar, y Terminar

INFINITIVES AND PAST FORMS

to begin	began
to continue	continued
to end	ended
to finish	finished

The present participle of *to begin* has two *n*'s (*beginning*).

INFINITIVOS

comenzar
continuar
terminar
terminar

El gerundio de *to begin* tiene dos *n*'s (*beginning*).

SENTENCES

Repeat with your teacher.

> He **finished** the chair.
> They **began** to work.
> She **continued** her studies.
> It **was beginning** to rain.
> The movie **ended** sadly.
> I **finished** my painting.
> We **could**n't **finish** our food.

> Please **finish** your test.
> **Begin** on the top line.
> **Continue** your work tomorrow.
> **Don't begin** yet.

> **Did** you **begin** on Tuesday?
> Yes, I **did**.

> What time **did** the show **end**?
> It **ended** at seven.

> **Did**n't they **finish** yesterday?
> No, they **did**n't.

Finished, began, and *continued* are often used with *ing* words. In these cases, the *ing* words are not part of the verb.

EXAMPLES (EJEMPLOS):
She finished painting the doors.
He continued studying.
They began working here last month.

ORACIONES

Repita con su maestro o maestra.

Finished, began y *continued* se usan frecuentemente con palabras que terminan con *ing*. En estos casos, las palabras con *ing* no son parte del verbo.

EXERCISE 1

Change these sentences to the past tense.

EJERCICIO 1

Cambie estas oraciones al pretérito.

    1. Sandra begins to read.

----

    2. We continue talking.

----

    3. They finish washing the dishes.

----

    4. The music ends.

----

    5. The cook finishes early.

----

    6. It continues to rain.

----

    7. We begin to play.

----

    8. The carnival ends on Tuesday.

EXERCISE 2

Write sentences using commands. Use the words *finish, give, bring, continue,* and *begin*.

EJERCICIO 2

Escriba oraciones usando mandamientos. Use las palabras *finish, give, bring, continue,* y *begin*.

    1. ---

    2. ---

    3. ---

    4. ---

    5. ---

Review of Section VI

Repaso de Sección VI

EXERCISE 1

Write the past form beside each infinitive. Then write **R** if the verb is regular or **I** if it is irregular.

EJERCICIO 1

Escriba el pretérito al lado de cada infinitivo. Luego escriba **R** si el verbo es regular o **I** si es irregular.

1. to end _____ _____

2. to die _____ _____

3. to find _____ _____

4. to open _____ _____

5. to lose _____ _____

6. to continue _____ _____

7. to close _____ _____

8. to live _____ _____

9. to finish _____ _____

10. to ask _____ _____

11. to begin _____ _____

12. to answer _____ _____

EXERCISE 2

Write *command* if the sentence is a command, *question* if it is a question, or *statement* if it is a statement.

EJERCICIO 2

Escriba *command* si la oración es un mandamiento, *question* si es una pregunta, o *statement* si es una declaración.

1. He found his glasses. _____

2. Begin reading on the next page. _____

3. They lived in a small town. _____

4. Did you finish reading the paper? _____

5. Please close your books. _____

6. Ask the clerk for an application form. _____

7. Where did they find it?   -

8. We lost our way.   -

9. Open the envelope carefully.   -

10. The meeting ended at eight.   -

EXERCISE 3

Cross out the incorrect word.

1. Did you (opened, open) my suitcase?
2. We were (lived, living) on a farm.
3. Was he (died, dying)?
4. I couldn't (answer, answered) the last question.
5. Please (closed, close) the door.
6. It (continued, continuing) snowing.
7. Where did you (lose, lost) it?
8. (Answered, Answer) all the questions, please.

EXERCISE 4

Write sentences using commands. Use the words *open, take, move, close, ask,* and *answer.*

EJERCICIO 3

Tache la palabra incorrecta.

EJERCICIO 4

Escriba oraciones usando mandamientos. Use las palabras *open, take, move, close, ask,* y *answer.*

1. -

2. -

3. -

4. -

5. -

6. -

SECTION VII
Verbs Dealing with Feelings

43. To Smile, To Laugh, and To Cry

INFINITIVES AND PAST FORMS

to smile   smiled
to laugh   laughed
to cry   cried

SENTENCES

Study the verbs carefully. Then repeat the sentences with your teacher.

I **cried** when I saw that movie.
The baby **was smiling**.
We **laughed** during the movie.
My child **was crying**.
They **smiled** for the picture.
Why **were** you **smiling**?
Don't laugh so loud.

Was the baby **crying**?
Yes, she **was**.

Were they **smiling**?
Yes, they **were**.

Did you **laugh** at his joke?
Yes, I **did**.

EXERCISE 1

Rewrite these sentences by using contractions.

1. Larry was not smiling.

SECCIÓN VII
Verbos sobre Sentimientos

43. Sonreír, Reírse, y Llorar

INFINITIVOS

sonreír
reírse
llorar

ORACIONES

Estudie los verbos cuidadosamente. Luego repita las oraciones con su maestra o maestro.

EJERCICIO 1

Escriba de nuevo estas oraciones usando contracciones.

2. He did not laugh very much.

----

3. She could not laugh.

----

4. They were not crying.

----

5. You were not laughing at all.

----

6. I did not cry.

EXERCISE 2

Complete the answers to the following questions by using the short form.

EJERCICIO 2

Complete las respuestas a las siguientes preguntas usando la forma corta.

1. Did she smile?

Yes, --

2. Were they laughing?

No, --

3. Was he able to smile?

Yes, --

4. Didn't you cry?

No, --

5. Was he smiling?

Yes, --

44. To Enjoy and To Complain

44. Gozar y Quejarse

INFINITIVES AND PAST FORMS

INFINITIVOS

to enjoy   enjoyed
to complain   complained

gozar
quejarse

Notice that the *y* in *enjoy* is not dropped in forming the past tense. This is because there is a vowel before the *y*.

Note que la *y* en *enjoy* no se elimina en formar el pretérito. Esto es porque hay una vocal antes de la *y*.

SENTENCES

ORACIONES

Repeat these sentences with your teacher.

Repita estas oraciones con su maestro o maestra.

We **enjoyed** the fiesta.
They **complained** about the noise.
I **enjoyed** the food.
Marta **was enjoying** the party.
You **were complaining** too much.
We **complained** to the manager.

Did you **enjoy** yourself?
Yes, I **did**.

Did he **complain** about anything?
No, he **did**n't.

Was she **complaining** to the attendant?
Yes, she **was**.

Enjoyed is sometimes used with *ing* words. The *ing* words are not part of the verb.

> EXAMPLE (EJEMPLO):
> I enjoyed working at that ranch.

Enjoyed se usa a veces con palabras que terminan con *ing*. Las palabras con *ing* no son parte del verbo.

EXERCISE 1

EJERCICIO 1

Cross out the incorrect word.

Tache la palabra incorrecta.

1. We (enjoying, enjoyed) our vacation.
2. Did you (enjoying, enjoy) your trip?
3. They (were, was) complaining about many things.
4. Why didn't he (complain, complained) to the owner?

5. Luisa and I (were, was) complaining about the smoke.
6. Why didn't you (enjoy, enjoyed) the picnic?

EXERCISE 2

Rewrite these sentences as questions.

EJERCICIO 2

Escriba de nuevo estas oraciones como preguntas.

1. He complained to the waiter.

---

2. They were enjoying the parade.

---

3. Laura enjoyed the show.

---

4. She was complaining about the poor lighting.

EXERCISE 3

Complete the answers to the following questions by using the short form.

EJERCICIO 3

Complete las respuestas a las siguientes oraciones usando la forma corta.

1. Did you enjoy your vacation?

   Yes, _____

2. Was she able to complain to the owner?

   Yes, _____

3. Didn't you enjoy the music?

   No, _____

4. Were they complaining again?

   No, _____

45. To Touch, To Feel, and To Hear

45. Tocar, Sentirse, y Oír

INFINITIVES AND PAST FORMS

to touch	touched
to feel	felt
to hear	heard

INFINITIVOS

tocar
sentirse
oír

SENTENCES

Repeat with your teacher.

They **felt** the material.
You **touched** the ceiling.
We **heard** a noise.
I **could**n't **touch** my toes.
We **felt** very tired.
She **heard** the crash.
We **were hearing** loud noises.
Touch the window, please.
Don't touch those wires.

Was he **feeling** sad?
No, he **was**n't.

Did they **touch** the statue?
No, they **did**n't.

Did she **hear** about the fire?
Yes, she **heard** about it.

ORACIONES

Repita con su maestra o maestro.

EXERCISE 1

Write sentences using the past or past progressive of *to touch*.

EJERCICIO 1

Escriba oraciones usando el pretérito o imperfecto de *to touch*.

1. _____

2. _____

3. _____

4. _____

5. _____

6. _____

7. --

8. --

EXERCISE 2

Write sentences using the past or past progressive of *to feel*.

EJERCICIO 2

Escriba oraciones usando el pretérito o imperfecto de *to feel*.

1. --

2. --

3. --

4. --

5. --

6. --

7. --

8. --

EXERCISE 3

Write sentences using the past or past progressive of *to hear*.

EJERCICIO 3

Escriba oraciones usando el pretérito o imperfecto de *to hear*.

1. --

2. --

3. --

4. --

5. --

6. --

7. --

8. --

46. To Decide, To Choose, and To Want

46. Decidir, Escoger, Querer, y Desear

INFINITIVES AND PAST FORMS

INFINITIVOS

to decide	decided
to choose	chose
to want	wanted

decidir
escoger
querer, desear

SENTENCES

ORACIONES

Repeat these sentences with your teacher.

Repita estas oraciones con su maestro o maestra.

They **decided** to go to Mexico this year.
I **chose** some apples from the fruit stand.
Helen **wanted** to study Spanish.
You **were choosing** the wrong color.
Steve **decided** to return home.
We **wanted** to go to the dance.
Please **choose** quickly.

Which jacket **did** you **choose**?
I **chose** the blue one.

Did you **decide** what to wear?
Yes, I **did**.

Did she **want** to work?
Yes, she **did**.

Where **did** he **decide** to go?
He **decided** to go to the movies.

EXERCISE 1

EJERCICIO 1

In the space beside each group of words, write the letter of the Spanish translation.

En el espacio al lado de cada grupo de palabras, escriba la letra de la traducción al español.

1. she chose   _____   a. ella estaba escogiendo

2. He was deciding.   _____   b. ella escogió

3. He couldn't decide. _____   c. Él no pudo decidir.

4. he wanted   _____   d. Ella no decidió.

5. she was choosing   _____   e. Él estaba decidiendo.

6. She didn't decide. _____   f. él quiso

EXERCISE 2

Complete the answers to the following questions by using the short form.

EJERCICIO 2

Complete las respuestas a las siguientes oraciones usando la forma corta.

1. Did you decide which color to get?

   Yes, _____

2. Did they want to leave?

   No, _____

3. Was she choosing wisely?

   Yes, _____

4. Did he want any coffee?

   No, _____

5. Were they deciding what to do?

   Yes, _____

6. Did he choose the large one?

   No, _____

EXERCISE 3

Write sentences using commands. Use the words *choose, touch, open, put,* and *give*.

EJERCICIO 3

Escriba oraciones usando mandamientos. Use las palabras *choose, touch, open, put,* y *give*.

1. _____

2. _____

3. _____

4. _____

5. _____

6. _____

7. _____

8. _____

9. _____

10. _____

47. To Like, To Love, and To Hope

47. Gustar, Amar, Querer, y Esperar

INFINITIVES AND PAST FORMS

to like	liked
to love	loved
to hope	hoped

INFINITIVOS

gustar
amar, querer
esperar

USAGE

The use of *gustar* in Spanish is very different from the use of *to like* in English. Consider the following sentences.

EXAMPLE (EJEMPLO):
Philip liked the music.   Le gustó la música a Felipe.

In the Spanish sentence, the word *música* is the subject of the sentence, and *Felipe* is the indirect object. In the English sentence, *Philip* is the subject and *music* is the object.

USO

El uso de *gustar* en español es muy diferente del uso de *to like* en inglés. Considere la siguientes oraciones.

En la oración en español, la palabra *música* es el sujeto de la oración, y *Felipe* es el objeto indirecto. En la oración en inglés, *Philip* es el sujeto y *music* es el objeto.

SENTENCES

Repeat with your teacher.

ORACIONES

Repita con su maestra o maestro.

She **liked** the show.
He **was hoping** for a promotion.
The children **liked** the circus.
They **loved** each other.
We **were hoping** for rain.
He **liked** to walk in the park.

Did he **love** her?
Yes, he **did**.

Were you **hoping** to see him?
Yes, I **was**.

Liked is sometimes used with *ing* words. The *ing* words are not part of the verb.

EXAMPLE (EJEMPLO):
She liked reading short stories.

Liked se usa a veces con palabras que terminan con *ing*. Las palabras con *ing* no son parte del verbo.

EXERCISE 1

Cross out the incorrect word.

1. Did you (liked, like) the movie?
2. They did (love, loved) their children.
3. I was (hoping, hoped) to go home early.
4. Why did he (like, liked) that story?
5. We (hoped, hoping) to earn a lot of money.
6. She (liked, liking) driving through the country.

EJERCICIO 1

Tache la palabra incorrecta.

EXERCISE 2

Fill in the blanks with the correct words.

1. We _____ _____ to see the movie
   estábamos   esperando
   again.

2. I _____ the food.
   me gustó

3. Did they _____ each other?
   amaron

4. He _____ his parents very much.
   amó

EJERCICIO 2

Llene los espacios con las palabras correctas.

EXERCISE 3

Write sentences using the past or past progressive of each of the following verbs at least once: *to love, to hope, to decide, to want,* and *to like.*

1. _____
2. _____
3. _____
4. _____
5. _____

EJERCICIO 3

Escriba oraciones usando el pretérito o imperfecto de cado uno de los siguientes verbos a lo menos una vez: *to love, to hope, to decide, to want,* y *to like.*

FIND THE VERBS

Find and circle the English translations of the following words. Some of the words are vertical, others are horizontal, and others are slanting. The first verb has already been circled.

ENCUENTRE LOS VERBOS

Encuentre y ponga un círculo alrededor de las traducciones al inglés de las siguientes palabras. Unas de las palabras están verticales, otras horizontales, y otras sesgadas. El primer verbo ya está circulado.

1. gozó
2. quiso
3. sonrió
4. esperó
5. lloró
6. amó
7. oyó
8. sentió
9. se quejó
10. escogió
11. se rió
12. le gustó
13. decidió

```
W L T V O C O D E B C L O F T E D A B
A D E S M I L E D E D L O V E D E Y X
N A U G O Y B C A P E R A Y U B O T Y
T A L V O N S I N N O V S U T A L O A
E M O H O P E D O S G H I N G I L P O
D A T G O C X E L O F A S M E H O N X
A P S Q I R E D B U D U N I E R E K O
C A L T X I B H E D O N N A T S O D I
E R S O T E Z N I X L O R B Q T I E L
U B O T T D J I R E B D G O R Y Z O X
B R E M F O Y K O C L A T E N I F E E
S A L A Y B U N N O S T L P A F O X A
L O B E F I G C O M P L A I N E D S I
I J D S E D O L H E R I B D G L H I A
K L E X A C H O S E J K O P R T U Q Q
X M G O N Z L K A R D E F I S T M I Y
O F E C H H E A Y E A D M O T N E D D
B L A G H P O V E N O T R A S M J A E
A B C D E F G H I J K L M N O P Q R S
```

Review of Section VII

EXERCISE 1

Write the past form beside each infinitive. Then write **R** if the verb is regular or **I** if it is irregular.

Repaso de Sección VII

EJERCICIO 1

Escriba el pretérito al lado de cada infinitivo. Luego escriba **R** si el verbo es regular o **I** si es irregular.

1. to want _____ _____

2. to smile _____ _____

3. to choose _____ _____

4. to hope _____ _____

5. to feel _____ _____

6. to laugh _____ _____

7. to touch _____ _____

8. to love _____ _____

9. to hear _____ _____

10. to like _____ _____

11. to cry _____ _____

12. to complain _____ _____

13. to decide _____ _____

14. to enjoy _____ _____

EXERCISE 2

Change these sentences to the past tense.

EJERCICIO 2

Cambie estas oraciones al pretérito.

1. She complains about the poor service.

   _____

2. I touch the leaves of the tree.

   _____

3. You enjoy the play.

   _____

4. He hears the bird singing.

----

5. We laugh very loudly.

----

6. They decide to go home.

EXERCISE 3

Change these sentences to the past progressive.

EJERCICIO 3

Cambie estas oraciones al imperfecto.

1. We enjoy the dance.

----

2. She smiles.

----

3. The children laugh at the cartoons.

----

4. The baby cries softly.

----

5. They complain about the bad weather.

----

6. I feel dizzy.

EXERCISE 4

Cross out the incorrect word.

EJERCICIO 4

Tache la palabra incorrecta.

1. Did they (enjoyed, enjoy) visiting their relatives?
2. Which one did he (choose, chose)?
3. Do not (touched, touch) the iron.
4. They (were, was) laughing very loud.
5. I (hearing, heard) the train whistle.

TEST ON SECTION I   (EXAMEN DE SECCIÓN I)

Name *(Nombre)* ....

Date *(Fecha)* .... Score *(Cuenta)* ....

A   Change these sentences to the past tense.
   Cambie estas oraciones al pretérito.

1. She knows how to paint.

   ----

2. They speak with their landlord.

   ----

3. I forget the date.

   ----

4. You understand the lesson.

   ----

5. We listen to the bird singing.

   ----

6. He learns how to cook.

   ----

7. Manuel teaches me how to play the guitar.

   ----

8. She writes very clearly.

   ----

9. They translate the story into French.

   ----

10. He talks about his children.

   ----

11. She reads the pamphlet.

Maximum Score 44 (4 points each)   Score ....
Cuenta Máxima 44 (4 puntos cada uno)   *Cuenta*

1

B   Fill in each blank with **was** or **were**.

*Llene cada espacio con **was** o **were**.*

1. I _____ captain of the team.

2. They _____ not at the dance.

3. She _____ a very good singer.

4. You _____ a good host.

5. It _____ very late.

6. We _____ not tired.

7. He _____ at the meeting.

8. They _____ not at home.

Maximum Score 32 (4 points each)   Score _____

Cuenta Máxima 32 (4 puntos cada uno)   *Cuenta*

C   Rewrite these sentences by using contractions.

Escriba de nuevo estas oraciones usando contracciones.

1. She was not happy.

    ----

2. They were not at the meeting.

    ----

3. You were not alone.

    ----

4. I was not ill.

    ----

5. We were not hungry.

    ----

6. It was not very large.

Maximum Score 24 (4 points each)   Score _____

Cuenta Máxima 24 (4 puntos cada uno)   *Cuenta*

2

TEST ON SECTION II (EXAMEN DE SECCIÓN II)

Name (*Nombre*) ....

Date (*Fecha*) .... Score (*Cuenta*) ....

A   Change these sentences to the past tense.
Cambie estas oraciones al pretérito.

    1. We clean our tools.

    ----

    2. Javier and Sara eat some cookies.

    ----

    3. She does her work quickly.

    ----

    4. I make a mistake.

    ----

    5. You rest very little.

    ----

    6. They help us paint our house.

    ----

    7. He washes the windows.

    ----

    8. We cook breakfast.

Maximum Score 40 (5 points each)   Score ....
Cuenta Máxima 40 (5 puntos cada uno)   *Cuenta*

B   Rewrite these sentences as negative sentences by using **did not** or **didn't**.
*Escriba de nuevo estas oraciones como oraciones negativas usando **did not** o **didn't**.*

    1. I slept very well last night.

    ----

2. Juanita ate her food.

----

3. We cleaned the classroom.

----

4. You washed your hands.

----

5. The baby drank the milk.

----

6. He helped us carry the grocery bags.

Maximum Score 30 (5 points each)   Score _____
Cuenta Máxima 30 (5 puntos cada uno)   *Cuenta*

C   Rewrite these sentences by using **did** to give more emphasis.

*Escriba de nuevo estas oraciones usando **did** para dar más énfasis.*

1. I cooked the food.

----

2. The children cleaned their room.

----

3. He woke up very early.

----

4. She washed all the clothes.

----

5. They helped us yesterday.

----

6. You slept too much.

Maximum Score 30 (5 points each)   Score _____
Cuenta Máxima 30 (5 puntos cada uno)   *Cuenta*

TEST ON SECTION III   (EXAMEN DE SECCIÓN III)

Name *(Nombre)* ....

Date *(Fecha)* .... Score *(Cuenta)* ....

A   Rewrite the following sentences as questions by using **did**.

*Escriba de nuevo las siguientes oraciones como preguntas usando **did**.*

1. He counted all of the boxes.

   ----

2. She had the answer.

   ----

3. Judy kept the keys to the house.

   ----

4. He spent all of his paycheck.

   ----

5. They sold their television set.

   ----

6. It cost a lot of money.

   ----

7. Alberto bought a new rug for his house.

Maximum Score 35 (5 points each)   Score ....
Cuenta Máxima 35 (5 puntos cada uno)   *Cuenta*

B   Answer the following questions in the positive. Answer with the verb in the past tense.

Conteste las siguientes oraciones en el positivo. Conteste con el verbo en el pretérito.

1. Did they save their coupons?

   ----

2. Did Elena work last Wednesday?

   ----

3. Did you pay the rent?

----

4. Did he owe money to the hospital?

----

5. Did she have the books?

----

6. Did she buy that sewing machine?

----

7. Did that fruit cost very little?

Maximum Score 35 (5 points each)   Score _____
Cuenta Máxima 35 (5 puntos cada uno)   *Cuenta*

C   Answer the following questions. Use **did** and the basic form of the verb for the first three questions and **didn't** and the basic form of the verb for questions 4-6.

*Conteste las siguientes preguntas. Use **did** y la forma básica del verbo para las primeras tres oraciones y **didn't** y la forma básica del verbo para oraciones 4-6.*

1. Did she save her stamps?

----

2. Did Paul work in a store?

----

3. Did you buy the groceries?

----

4. Did they sell the old car?

----

5. Did you keep the pliers?

----

6. Did Lupe pay the utilities?

Maximum Score 30 (5 points each)   Score _____
Cuenta Máxima 30 (5 puntos cada uno)   *Cuenta*

6

TEST ON SECTION IV   (EXAMEN DE SECCIÓN IV)

Name (Nombre) ....

Date (Fecha) .... Score (Cuenta) ....

A   Fill in the blanks with the correct words.

Llene los espacios con las palabras correctas.

1. Ricardo .... a pickup.
   estaba   conduciendo

2. We .... at a very nice hotel.
   nos quedamos

3. He .... not cut the meat with that knife.
   pudo

4. They .... their relatives in
   estaban   visitando

   Mexico.

5. You .... the party very early.
   salió

6. Beatriz .... her nephew to class.
   trajo

7. The bus .... late.
   llegó

8. They .... by boat.
   estaban   viajando

9. I .... the papers home.
   llevé

10. We .... to the library to study.
    fuimos

11. Juan and César .... to school early.
    vinieron

Maximum Score 44 (4 points each sentence)   Score ....
Cuenta Màxima 44 (4 puntos cada oración)   *Cuenta*

B   Change these sentences from the present to the past progressive.

Cambie estas oraciones del presente al imperfecto.

1. She walks home.

....

2. They wait for class to begin.

----

3. I use the saw.

----

4. Michael and Ken leave in the morning.

----

5. She visits her aunt.

----

6. I change my clothes.

----

7. You call your parents.

----

8. They take a test.

Maximum Score 32 (4 points each)   Score ....
Cuenta Máxima 32 (4 puntos cada uno)   *Cuenta*

C   Rewrite the following sentences by using contractions.
     Escriba de nuevo las siguientes oraciones usando contracciones.

1. I was not using your pen.

----

2. They could not come to school.

----

3. We were not able to wait any longer.

----

4. We were not bringing our books.

Maximum Score 24 (6 points each)   Score ....
Cuenta Máxima 24 (6 puntos cada uno)   *Cuenta*

TEST ON SECTION V   (EXAMEN DE SECCIÓN V)

Name (Nombre) ....

Date (Fecha) .... Score (Cuenta) ....

A   Fill in the blanks with the correct words.

Llene los espacios con las palabras correctas.

1. He .... a medal during the war.
   recibió

2. I .... for my other shoe.
   estaba   buscando

3. They .... the transmission
   estaban   reparando
   in the car.

4. The window .... because of the noise.
   se quebró

5. We .... down to eat.
   nos sentamos

6. She .... at the beautiful sunset.
   estaba   mirando

7. Claudia and María .... to learn
   estaban   tratando
   English.

8. The sail in the boat ....
   se rompió

9. He didn't .... us enter his house.
   dejó

10. I .... the papers on top of the desk.
    puse

11. You .... about the size of the box.
    estaba   mintiendo

12. We .... that movie two times.
    vimos

Maximum Score 48 (4 points each sentence)   Score ....
Cuenta Máxima 48 (4 puntos cada oración)   Cuenta

B   Rewrite these sentences as positive questions in the past progressive.

Escriba de nuevo estas oraciones como preguntas positivas en el imperfecto.

1. You were trying to talk to the manager.

....

9

2. She was looking for her notebook.

----

3. They were receiving the morning paper.

----

4. He was thinking of enlisting in the army.

----

5. The dog was lying down.

----

6. You were fixing this chair.

----

7. She was giving them music lessons.

----

8. They were getting tired.

Maximum Score 16 (2 points each)   Score _____
Cuenta Máxima 16 (2 puntos cada uno)   *Cuenta*

C   Cross out the incorrect word.
    Tache la palabra incorrecta.

1. Did you (get, got) my letter?
2. She (laid, lay) the bags on the floor this morning.
3. They (were, was) thinking of going to the park.
4. I could (saw, see) the car.
5. I (lay down, lied down) to go to sleep.
6. He (thanked, thought) about the problem.
7. She (set, sat) the table.
8. We (put, sat) the flowers on the table.
9. He didn't tell the truth. He (lied down, lied).
10. She (placed, sat) on the chair.
11. The machine (broke, tore).
12. The tailor (broke, tore) the material in two.

Maximum Score 36 (3 points each)   Score _____
Cuenta Máxima 36 (3 puntos cada uno)   *Cuenta*

10

TEST ON SECTION VI   *(EXAMEN DE SECCIÓN VI)*

Name *(Nombre)* ....

Date *(Fecha)* .... Score *(Cuenta)* ....

A   Change these sentences from the present to the past or from the present progressive to the past progressive.

Cambie estas oraciones del presente al pretérito o del presente progresivo al imperfecto.

1. They are living in Mexico.

   ----

2. The old man is dying.

   ----

3. It begins to rain.

   ----

4. He opens the package.

   ----

5. I lose my sweater.

   ----

6. You answer the phone.

   ----

7. She is asking for permission to leave.

   ----

8. The fire continues to burn.

   ----

9. The show ends at three.

   ----

10. Mark finds the word in the dictionary.

    ----

11. They finish their work.

    ----

12. The police close the road.

Maximum Score 48 (4 points each)   Score _____
Cuenta Máxima 48 (4 puntos cada uno)   *Cuenta*

B   Write six sentences using commands. Use the following words.

       Escriba seis oraciones con mandamientos. Use las siguientes palabras.

       open   begin   ask
       close   continue   answer

       1. ---

       2. ---

       3. ---

       4. ---

       5. ---

       6. ---

Maximum Score 24 (4 points each)   Score _____
Cuenta Máxima 24 (4 puntos cada uno)   *Cuenta*

C   Write **statement** if the sentence is a statement, **command** if it is a command, or **question** if it is a question.

       *Escriba **statement** si la oración es una declaración, **command** si es un mandamiento, o **question** si es una pregunta.*

       1. Did you close the back door?   ----------------------------------

       2. Don't lose your papers.   ----------------------------------

       3. Please ask him if he can help us.   ----------------------------------

       4. They began to sing.   ----------------------------------

       5. Did they finish on time?   ----------------------------------

       6. Please open this jar for me.   ----------------------------------

       7. Were they living in an apartment?   ----------------------------------

Maximum Score 28 (4 points each)   Score _____
Cuenta Máxima 28 (4 puntos cada uno)   *Cuenta*

TEST ON SECTION VII (EXAMEN DE SECCIÓN VII)

Name (Nombre) _____

Date (Fecha) _____ Score (Cuenta) _____

A   Fill in the blanks with the correct words.

Llene los espacios con las palabras correctas.

1. Did you _____ when you saw the movie?
se rió

2. They _____ _____ about the
se estaban   quejando
poor service.

3. We _____ _____ to go fishing.
estábamos   esperando

4. Gilbert _____ the food at the fiesta.
le gustó

5. Please don't _____ the iron.
toque

6. She _____ a little tired.
se sintió

7. We _____ listening to the music.
gozamos

8. Did Juanita _____ which coat to buy?
escogió

9. I _____ to play soccer with my friend.
quise

10. You _____ _____ when they took that
estaba   sonriendo
picture.

11. The child _____ _____.
estaba   llorando

12. They _____ a loud sound.
oyeron

Maximum Score 36 (3 points each sentence)   Score _____
Cuenta Máxima 36 (3 puntos cada oración)   *Cuenta*

B   Cross out the incorrect word.

Tache la palabra incorrecta.

1. Please (don't, didn't) complain so much.

2. Why (were, was) they crying?

3. (Did, Were) you enjoying the show?

4. You (were, was) laughing very loudly.

5. (Did, Were) you hoping to see that movie?

6. I did (love, loved) my parents very much.

7. Why did they (want, wanted) to go?

8. Lucy and Rita (was, were) touching the material.

9. She (decide, decided) not to go to class.

10. Please (choose, chose) quickly.

11. (Were, Was) they touching those hot pipes?

12. I did (liked, like) the dance.

Maximum Score 36 (3 points each)   Score _____
Cuenta Máxima 36 (3 puntos cada uno)   *Cuenta*

C   Complete the answers to these questions by using the short form.
     Complete las respuestas a estas preguntas usando la forma corta.

1. Did you hear the dog howling?

   Yes, _____

2. Were they hoping to go to the bank in the morning?

   Yes, _____

3. Did she like the story?

   No, _____

4. Was he complaining about the noise?

   No, _____

5. Didn't you laugh when you heard the joke?

   No, _____

6. Did they want to go with us?

   Yes, _____

7. Was he able to decide quickly?

   Yes, _____

Maximum Score 28 (4 points each)   Score _____
Cuenta Máxima 28 (4 puntos cada uno)   *Cuenta*

14

FINAL TEST   (EXAMEN FINAL)

Name (Nombre) ....

Date (Fecha) .... Score (Cuenta) ....

A   Cross out the incorrect word.
     Tache la palabra incorrecta.

1. Did you (saw, see) the race?

2. They (laid, lay) the bricks on the floor yesterday.

3. (Were, Was) you going to the hardware store?

4. Please (answer, answered) the phone.

5. Jerry and I (were, was) working in the same department.

6. They didn't (knew, know) the answer to that question.

7. We couldn't (move, moved) the statue.

8. Why did he (leave, left) so early?

9. Don't (write, wrote) on the other side of the paper.

10. Please (give, gave) me that book.

Maximum Score 40 (4 points each)   Score ....
Cuenta Máxima 40 (4 puntos cada uno)   *Cuenta*

B   Change the sentences in the past tense to questions in the past tense.
     Change the sentences in the past progressive to questions in the past
     progressive.
     *Cambie las oraciones en el pretérito a preguntas en el pretérito. Cambie las
     oraciones en el imperfecto a preguntas en el imperfecto.*

1. She wrote her name at the top of the page.

   ----

2. They were living in a two-bedroom apartment.

   ----

3. He was walking to the store.

   ----

4. They paid off the loan on the car.

Maximum Score 20 (5 points each)   Score ....
Cuenta Máxima 20 (5 puntos cada uno)   *Cuenta*

C　Complete the answers to the following questions. Use any form you wish.

Complete las respuestas a las siguientes oraciones. Use cualquiera forma que Ud. desea.

　　1. Did they go to the post office?

　　　Yes, _____

　　2. Could he open the jar?

　　　No, _____

　　3. Were you looking for me?

　　　Yes, _____

　　4. Did she go to work yesterday?

　　　Yes, _____

　　5. Did he forget to get his license plates?

　　　No, _____

　　6. Could she translate the story?

　　　Yes, _____

Maximum Score 24 (4 points each)　　　　　　　　　　　　Score _____
Cuenta Máxima 24 (4 puntos cada uno)　　　　　　　　　*Cuenta*

D　Write eight sentences using commands. Use the following words.

Escriba ocho oraciones con mandamientos. Use las siguientes palabras.

give	bring	help	leave
put	move	open	take

　　1. _____

　　2. _____

　　3. _____

　　4. _____

　　5. _____

　　6. _____

　　7. _____

　　8. _____

Maximum Score 16 (2 points each)　　　　　　　　　　　　Score _____
Cuenta Máxima 16 (2 puntos cada uno)　　　　　　　　　*Cuenta*

16